D0323697

The
Weekend
Dog

The Weekend Dog

Myrna M. Milani, D.V.M.

Illustrations by
Pamela Carroll

RAWSON ASSOCIATES : New York

to
Jim, Jeremy, and Dan
with love

Library of Congress Cataloging in Publication Data

Milani, Myrna, M.
   The weekend dog.

   Includes index.
   1. Dogs. I. Title.
SF427.M54   1984   636.7   83–42629
ISBN 0-89256-252-8

Contents

List of Illustrations

Acknowledgments

The Weekend Dog could not have been written without the help and support of these very special individuals:

My parents Marie and Henry Morth who, "in spite of everything," let me get that first dog that changed my life.

My colleagues, clients and patients at the Cheshire Animal Hospital, especially friends Ann Foley, Kerry Beverstock, and Steve Frye, who help me keep the balance between animals and people.

Marjorie Zerbel, who typed on short notice and always with good humor.

Mike Snell, who thinks like a dog and edits like a saint.

Brian Smith, who gives me the courage to change those things I can, the serenity to accept those I cannot, and the love and wisdom to know the difference.

Before You Begin
This Book

On their way back to New York from their summer home in Vermont, Dick and Sally Burgess abandon their six-month old elkhound at a rest area in Connecticut. The dog's chewing and roaming were bad enough at their rustic camp, but this behavior can't be tolerated in their new Westchester condominium.

A widowered accountant with heart problems stares silently through the window of his apartment at the empty street below. He didn't realize he would miss his yappy little terrier so much. But his landlord said it was him or the dog, and a good apartment is hard to replace. What choice did he have? Unfortunately, his choice may very well shorten his own life.

Since 1978 more than 55 million healthy dogs have met death in humane societies and animal shelters across the United States, and countless more have been put to sleep by veterinarians. What bothers me most about this alarming statistic is the fact that these animals do not just represent a national epidemic of unwanted puppies and strays. Many are animals someone wanted and probably loved at one time, dogs from the best kennels and homes; big, little, smart, and dumb dogs that belonged to all kinds of people like you and me. Each year, millions of dogs are being abandoned, conveniently lost, given away, or deliberately put down because they just didn't work out, just couldn't successfully fit into their working owners' lives.

In many cases, people could have changed that. My experience has taught me that dogs don't work out for two basic reasons: (1) people don't always understand their dogs, and (2) dogs don't always understand their people. We may have progressed far from the caves and the wolf pack, but we've also come a long way from the days when Mom, or someone, was home twenty-four hours a day, seven days a week to create and maintain that perfect house pet of our youth.

Like it or not, most of us now work or spend a fair amount of time away from home and end up cramming our home lives into evenings and weekends. Although the majority of American dogs stay home all day, most owner/ dog interaction occurs in those evening and weekend hours. The traditional dog of ten years ago has evolved into the weekend dog of today. I learned this the hard way when I struggled to train my first weekend dog, Dufie. At the time, I thought my complex life-style combining family life, full-time job, and dog ownership was the exception. I thought I was the only person having trouble training a pup, the only parent cleaning up shredded rugs and houseplants every evening, the only person with a six-month-old pup that still was not housebroken. I eventually came to understand that all this physical and emotional chaos developed because those of us who spend a lot of time away from home form a different relationship and experience different problems with our dogs from what all the other dog books describe. It was not better, not worse, just different, and sufficiently so that we weekend dog owners must reexamine our beliefs and techniques and develop new ones to supplement or replace the old ones if necessary.

The Weekend Dog doesn't insist that either our life-style or our relationship with our dogs is wrong. Rather, it addresses those relationships between dogs and owners that may precipitate problems, offering specific cures for the most common ones. It treats the beautiful bond between dog and owner with respect and admiration, even when that bond has resulted in seemingly bizarre behavior. The mutual desire of people and dogs to love and need each other not only adds to the quality of life for both species, but it can also provide the key to resolving many contemporary canine problems. *The Weekend Dog* shows how to exploit the flexibility and strength of this bond and disengage ourselves from the crushing guilt that can surround our relationships with our pets in every stage of dog ownership, from housebreaking to death.

Even though our dogs may appear at times to add more confusion to a life-style that cries out for order, we won't give them up. *The Weekend Dog* proves that we don't have to, nor do we have to give up our furniture, our yards, or our good relationships with our neighbors. In the following pages you will learn how, in spite of what at times appear to be overwhelming odds, you can build and enjoy a rewarding relationship with your weekend dog.

CHAPTER 1

The Weekend Society and the Weekend Dog

John Dunn works five days a week as a computer programmer at Hohum Electronics. Ebony, his male black Labrador, always ran loose because John believes dogs should be free; but John's work schedule prevented him from spending sufficient time to teach the dog his boundaries or to come when called. Last winter, Ebony was legally shot by a game warden while running deer.

Eleanor Rossman got Clover, a female cocker spaniel, for companionship when all her children had grown and left home. Eleanor cooks filet mignon for Clover, grooms her with a special brush, and walks her whenever the dog goes to the door. When Eleanor eats, Clover eats; when Eleanor sleeps, Clover sleeps under the covers between Eleanor and her husband.

Steve and Joanie Bennet's friends think they're crazy. They live in a tiny apartment with their eighty-pound German shepherd, Colonel. From seven in the morning until five-thirty at night, Monday through Friday, Colonel sleeps in a fiber glass kennel just big enough for him, a blanket, and his favorite toy.

Weekend Dogs Belong to Weekend People

What is a weekend dog? Quite simply, a weekend dog is the canine member of what for many Americans has become a weekend way of life. We tend to adhere to one schedule Monday through Friday, but completely abandon it on Saturday and Sunday. Although the actual hours and days may differ, most of us have at least two patterns of life-style, even if only for a couple of weeks a year when we're on vacation; few people follow the same routine every day, 365 days a year, year in and year out.

In the past when the dog got sick, Mom took it to the vet's during the day. When a weekend dog gets sick, someone may have to stay home from work to take it to the vet's. Or Mom may have to rush home right after class to medicate it, missing an important meeting. And when the weekend dog suddenly starts chewing up the rug, it's more than a question of discipline. How can you discipline your dog if you're not home? What caused such behavior after five nondestructive years?

How do you know if you're a prospective or existing weekend dog owner? If your life-style is characterized by one or more of the following, you probably belong to the club:

- There is no one at your home for three to eight hours almost every day.
- Your dog spends twenty to sixty hours alone per week.

- You tend to have at least two patterns of life-style: one that involves outside employment, volunteer work, or other pursuits and another for weekends, holidays, or vacations.
- On any given weekday, you are as likely to be away from home as not.
- You don't adhere to the same schedule or routine seven days a week.

Three Traditional Beliefs About Dogs

To understand the weekend dog, we must understand the traditional dog, or rather traditional ideas about what constitutes a good dog. Like all pack animals, dogs exhibit consistent, predictable needs. If you want to keep a dog happy, you keep it company and fulfill its needs in a predictable, consistent manner. Simple? Not quite. It may have been simple in early rural America or even in the 1950s and early '60s because someone usually was at home. But today no one is home part or all of most days in as many as 75 percent of American homes—except the dog. And even when weekend owners are home, they want desperately to relax, to abandon the rigid order that often characterizes the daily work environment. Goodbye consistency and predictability.

Whether your dog is a Yorkshire terrier or a Saint Bernard, whether you hold down two jobs to make ends meet, spend a few hours a week at the country club, or do volunteer work at a local nursing home, you probably don't relate to your dog the way your parents did. Whereas your mother probably lived around the clock with faithful Flame underfoot, your own schedule makes that impossible. Dogs will happily transfer their pack instincts from other dogs to people, but dogs become unhappy, frustrated, and bored when their people are gone. Unhappy

dogs display a wide range of behavioral and medical problems that make their owners feel even more unhappy or,
worse, guilty about leaving their dogs alone. Misery feeds
on misery until the situation becomes intolerable, and the
owner abandons the pet or has it put to sleep. Consequently, an increasing number of us are finding ourselves
in an uncomfortable position with our dogs. If we judge
ourselves according to traditional beliefs, we must see ourselves as failures, but guilt seldom helps solve a problem.
On the other hand, we can change our beliefs about dogs
and ourselves and what is right for both of us. Let's examine the three most common beliefs people hold about the
role of dogs in our world.

Dogs Will Be Dogs—
The Independent Development Belief

The first traditional belief maintains that dogs are a separate species that evolved from ancient wolves, more or
less independent of human evolution. We will refer to this
view as the Independent Development belief. The Independent Development crowd considers people an interference, a dilution of the purity of ideal dogs. They often say
things like:

"Dogs should run free."
"Neutering dogs is unnatural."
"Dogs can take care of themselves."
"Dogs will be dogs."

Dogs Are People, Too!—
The Dependent Development Belief

Proponents of this belief insist that their dogs will eat
only table food, and they refer to their pets as one would
a person, usually a slightly backward child. These people
project their own traits and emotions on their dogs, using
such phrases as "What's good for me is good for my dog!"

and "Dogs are people, too!" Advocates of this Dependent Development view believe dogs react to pain, hunger, emotion, other people, and animals much the same way their owners do. To them, a dog's happiness is based on human values.

It's You and Me, Bruno—
The Bonded Development Belief

The third belief insists that canine and human evolution are inextricably intertwined. People aren't messing up dogs or vice versa, nor can dogs be considered as people. Rather, people and dogs are progressing simultaneously toward some common, albeit currently undefined, goal without losing their individual identity.

Those who hold the Bonded Development view recognize that dogs do things we don't always understand and we undoubtedly do things our dogs don't understand. However, they don't necessarily define such things as wrong. And even if they do—"I don't like it when my dog brings home a baby rabbit," they may say, or, "My dog doesn't like it when he's left alone for hours"—it doesn't undermine their love and respect for each other.

All these views are popular and their adherents can marshal ample proof to support each. However, many of the problems currently besetting the dog-owning population grow out of the fact that Independent or Dependent attitudes don't suit weekend life-styles well. Sick weekend dogs can no more fend for themselves than most weekend dog owners can afford to take days off from work to nurse them back to health. A dog that suddenly begins chewing the rug when the owner goes to work will not comprehend being banished to the outdoors after having slept on the couch for five years without consequence. In short, Independent views only work when the dog's uncontrolled behavior does not conflict with people. And Dependent views work only when someone stays home around the clock. For the busy weekend dog owner, neither view can work.

On the other hand, the Bonded view recognizes the variability of both people and dogs and also our *need* for each other. Because our weekend life-style is often characterized by great variability, which at times seems to intensify our need for love and companionship, the Bonded view readily fits into weekend life-styles. Let's look at a few examples of how these different orientations can clash or harmonize with the weekend dog.

Recognizing and Solving Dog-Owner Relationship Problems

If we ask John Dunn why his black Lab was shot chasing deer, John will probably shrug his shoulders and say, "You know how dogs are. Besides, I could never chain a dog. Dogs are born to run." However, John's life-style does not allow him to create an environment where his dog can operate safely within John's Independent belief. Ebony fell victim to undisciplined canine instincts; some dogs naturally chase other animals and will even bite them. But when Ebony's undisciplined instincts, supported by John's Independent beliefs, result in the dog's running winter-weakened deer to death, the game warden and the State of New Hampshire overruled them.

Whether John and Ebony, or the deer and the game warden, are right matters less than the fact that the traditional Independent Development view can get a weekend dog owner into a lot of trouble. Let's look at another case where an Independent belief causes a problem.

Sally Cargill works from four to midnight as a hostess at an inn in Gloucester, Massachusetts. When she and her husband divorced, Sally chose to remain in their secluded farmhouse; she also decided to get Jupiter, a Doberman, to protect the property in her absence. Every time the dog barked or growled at anything, Sally praised what she considered his protective behavior. Then one day Sally moved Jupiter's food dish while the dog was eating, and Jupiter mangled her arm from elbow to wrist. As soon as the mandatory ten-day restraint period ended, Sally had the dog put to sleep.

This problem began when Sally reinforced strong Independent territorial behavior in her dog without maintaining sufficient control over him. Her own fears allowed the dog to determine what was threatening to *both* of them, and she let the dog become the leader of their pack of two. Consequently, the simple act of moving Jupiter's food dish challenged that leadership, and the dog responded as a wild dog would: he bit. After supporting Jupiter's Independent behavior, Sally expected him to function as a wild, independent species with everyone *except* her; she wanted him to be her companion, to bond with her. But it doesn't work that way. Dogs, like people, need consistency. We cannot reinforce wild dog behavior one day, then expect the same dog to be our good buddy the next.

How about Dependent views? Eleanor Rossman's "little girl," Clover, didn't pose a problem until Eleanor's husband retired and the couple embarked on several long-postponed trips. The first time they boarded Clover, the cocker damaged the kennel to the tune of over a hundred dollars. Because of her destructive behavior and incessant howling, no kennel will take her now, so when the Rossmans travel, they must hire a dog-sitter. Even so, the unhappy dog continually paces and refuses to eat.

Having defined Clover as a highly dependent furry *person,* Eleanor now finds herself paying the consequences of the Dependent view. Furthermore, she must deal with the frustration and guilt her dog's behavior causes. Both pet and owner suffer.

Eleanor's choices in this situation are the same as John Dunn's and Sally Cargill's. She can:

(1) fatalistically accept the situation and her feelings about it,
(2) terminate the relationship (i.e., get rid of the dog), or
(3) change her beliefs and/or alter the dog's behavior.

What we or our dogs did in the past matters less than what we're going to do in the future to establish a harmonious relationship. If John had taken the time to teach Ebony his boundaries or have the pup professionally trained, Ebony could have run free within a limited area. Had Sally trained Jupiter to consistently respond to even the most basic come, sit, and stay commands, she would have given him confidence as well as teaching him to respect her. This combination of confidence and respect would have resulted in a pet Sally could always trust as well as depend on for protection. For Eleanor and Clover to be happy, Clover must learn to be a dog again, to gain confidence in herself as a nonhuman being so she can tolerate not being treated like the family baby. An overly dependent dog is an untrained, miserable pet. Here again, even the simplest obedience training can build vital confidence in both dog and owner. By communicating with Clover as a dog rather than a child, Eleanor begins to develop the unique human/dog bond. When she teaches Clover to come, sit, and stay, Eleanor creates a less dependent, more adaptable, and much happier pet—and, of course, when Clover is happy, Eleanor is happy.

Remember Colonel, who spends fifty hours a week in a fiber glass kennel? Well, Steve and Joanie Bennet's friends may think they're crazy, but the Bennets realize that Colonel's destructive behavior when left alone could ruin their relationship with their dog. Once they learn that Colonel's behavior is neither vicious nor spiteful, they find it much easier to accept the idea of kenneling him without guilt.

By understanding his needs as well as their own, they've worked out an acceptable solution to a most frustrating weekend dog problem.

In the next chapters we shall explore how our beliefs about dogs and their relation to us influence our pets' behavior, often creating problems that can be resolved only when we learn new attitudes and techniques.

CHAPTER 2

Selecting
a Weekend Dog

*M*ary MacComber's life revolves around her male beagle, Ashley, who reminds Mary of the dogs she grew
up with on a Missouri dairy farm. Ashley always behaves
like a perfect gentleman.

Dean Jameson got his female Gordon setter, Daphne,
two years ago. Since then the dog has been nothing but
trouble. Although Daphne is spayed, she so aggressively
protects Dean's property that he can't trust her out of the
house. One neighbor has threatened to shoot the dog if
she bares her teeth at his children again.

Ted and Mary Jane Crowder got their standard poodle
because neither of them like dogs that shed. Last month
the dog's quarterly clip and grooming cost thirty dollars.
"That's a lot of money," Ted complained to the groomer.
"That's a lot of dog," replied the groomer.

Selecting a dog is one of the most important events in a potential weekend dog owner's life. When you say yes to the breeder, neighbor, or humane society employee, or the child who brings an endearing ball of fluff home from school, you're putting your whole life-style on the line. Such decisions, while joyous at the moment, mark the beginning of what can become a nightmare. Selecting any dog—but especially one destined to be a weekend dog—should never be spontaneous or excessively emotional. In this chapter we'll discuss some major biological and behavioral traits of different breeds in terms of how they may simplify or complicate our lives, but first a word about feelings.

Beliefs Affect How We Feel About Dogs

Some people refuse to acknowledge the existence of any dog that weighs less than forty pounds. "That's not a dog," they say, "that's a rat." Others are terrified of any dog weighing more than forty pounds. "That's not a dog; that's a wolf." Breeds such as German shepherds ("police dogs"), Dobermans ("killers"), collies ("Lassie"), or poodles ("sissies") also ignite strong emotions in some people. If Mary MacComber was badly bitten by a cocker spaniel when she was a child, she'll probably distrust them for the rest of her life; conversely, if she recalls many wonderful hours with the family beagle, she may never consider any other kind of pet. Are such personal considerations valid when selecting your dog? You bet they are.

Ignoring your strong feelings about the right dog for you can greatly complicate your life, especially if you have barely enough time to feed, groom, and exercise a dog. If you dislike anything about a certain kind of dog, you will find it hard to develop more than a weak relationship with it. Perhaps you love dogs but hate dog hair. What happens if you adopt a thick-coated husky that sheds constantly? If you're an active person who enjoys hiking and camping with your dog, a silky-coated Lhasa apso that attracts burrs like a magnet and requires painstaking grooming will probably be more of a headache than a companion. Owners who come home after a long workday to cope with active toddlers may become frustrated and angry with an exuberant big dog underfoot.

Although no ironclad rules for selecting the right dog exist, as a potential owner you should make a list of qualities you want in a pet. For example, Mary MacComber's list eventually led to the selection of her beagle, Ashley:

Small enough to pick up
Enthusiastic
Male
No grooming or clipping
Not white or all black
Two- to four-month-old pup

Someone interested in showing beagles for a hobby might expand that list:

Beagle
Not more than fifteen inches tall when full grown
Close, medium-length coat
Good markings
Championship show background
Good show personality

An avid weekend hunter might include:

Good nose
Vocal
Stamina
Strong body
Good hunting records both parents

Notice how dramatically these lists differ, because each reflects the tastes of the potential owner. Yet all three lists ultimately lead to the selection of the same breed.

Here's a list a couple of working parents compiled when choosing a companion for their allergic twelve-year-old.

Good-natured
Small
Minimal hair or dander
Enthusiastic but easily managed

Compare those traits to the characteristics sought by an avid weekend outdoorsman:

Over seventy pounds full-grown
Aggressive
Able to live outdoors year-round
Strong
Plenty of spirit

The former results in the selection of a Mexican hairless; the latter, a Malamute. Such lists, though not perfect guidelines, at least facilitate selection because they enable potential weekend dog owners to isolate certain major characteristics. If you have absolutely no idea where to begin, begin by listing those characteristics you definitely *don't* want. For many potential owners, this results in a short list but one that can narrow the field considerably. For example, Dean Jameson's list of canine dislikes includes:

No yappy little dogs
Nothing that has to be groomed
No males
No all-white dogs
No hounds
No herding dogs

He can immediately eliminate all the toy and miniature breeds, poodles, Old English sheepdogs and other breeds that require grooming, Samoyeds, Great Pyrenees, and other white breeds, beagles, Plott hounds, redbones, Black and Tans, coonhounds (scent hounds), shepherds, collies, shelties, and border collies (herding dogs), and all male animals, to name just a few. By using this process Dean arrived at a Gordon setter, Daphne.

This brings us to the one drawback in any selection process: sometimes, things don't work out no matter how hard we try. We can compile endless lists full of data, read all the breed books, and memorize all the standards—and still get a lemon. If you do, learn from the experience. Although Dean Jameson's careful selection process resulted in the troublesome Daphne, that doesn't necessarily mean Dean will have trouble with all Gordon setters. On the other hand, if Dean's experience makes him anti-Gordon setter, he'll probably be much better off avoiding all setters in the future. Learn to trust your feelings and select a dog that reflects your beliefs about dogs. We'll discuss beliefs in detail in Chapter 3, but for now, let's concentrate on the physical and behavioral dog traits that mean the most to the weekend owner.

Physical Traits:
Assets and Liabilities

Size

Dogs vary in weight from a few pounds (toy breeds) to over a hundred (Great Danes, Saint Bernards), but a typical dog weighs between twenty-five and forty pounds and enjoys a life-span of about twelve to thirteen years. Although we all know toy poodles or Great Danes that lived to twelve or fourteen, the very small and very large dogs tend to have shorter life-spans. When dogs are bred primarily for one trait, such as size, other traits often fall by the wayside. For example, when I see an eight-year-old toy poodle or Great Dane, I tend to treat them as I do twelve-year-old beagles or spaniels. Toy poodles are more prone to heart problems, epileptic seizures, and skeletal problems such as slipped disks and "trick knees," while Great Danes, because of size, more often fall victim to certain types of bone cancer.

Sex

Do females or males make better pets? It's largely a matter of experience and personal preference. People who have good experiences with one or the other will tend to think all dogs of that sex act like that. Although male dogs often live up to their own aggressive reputations, there are always exceptions within breeds. A normally placid female may become very aggressive when nursing pups. A young female springer spaniel living with her fourteen-year-old sire may develop typical male territorial behavior.

If you live in an area with a dense dog population, a spayed female will avoid many sex-related problems. Although spaying does not guarantee your dog won't be interested in other dogs or they in her, she probably will not disappear for days at a time like her intact (uncastrated) male counterparts.

When Mary MacComber got Ashley as a pup and moved into a condominium in suburban Chicago, there were few other dogs in the 150-unit complex. But soon there were more than sixty, so Mary opted to castrate Ashley when he was six months old. She says it's the best investment she ever made. Her neighbor's dog disappears every time a female dog goes into heat, something that seems to happen every other week, and he sometimes comes home bloody and battered from fighting. Because Mary and her neighbor car-pool, they've been late for work several times because they had to search for the wandering male.

Keep in mind that those traits characterizing male or female behavior in a pack or group situation may completely disappear in a household where there is only one dog, or in an area where few dogs live together. Dogs mark their territory by urinating or defecating, whether it's the back fence or the French Provincial chaise longue, to signal boundaries to other dogs, not people. If there are no other dogs around, such behavior may never occur. On the other hand, behavior that would never be tolerated within the pack, such as incessant howling or whining, may crop up in the single-pet household. Although typical male and female behavior does exist, it is not sufficiently predictable to rule out what might otherwise be your ideal weekend dog.

Coat

Even though ironclad rules seldom apply to dogs, you can count on having to groom any dog that doesn't shed. Do you shudder at the thought of vacuuming up balls of dog hair after a long day at work? Then consider a Lhasa or a poodle and spend that half hour every night combing out mats and tangles instead. If that's too much hassle, have it done professionally, and end up spending as much for your dog's grooming as you would for your own. Even a minimal grooming schedule of twice yearly at thirty dollars a clip can equal a lot of vacuum cleaner bags. If you enjoy grooming your pet or don't mind paying for professional grooming, breeds such as poodles, Lhasa apsos, or Bedlington, Yorkshire, or Scottish terriers may suit you well.

A lot of potential owners admire the primitive northern breeds, such as huskies, Malamutes, and Samoyeds, which possess many appealing characteristics, such as stamina, strength, and beauty. They also have extremely thick coats designed to protect them in bitterly cold climates. When these dogs shed, they set Guinness records. Their shedding is called "puffing" because great puffs of downy undercoat fall away. This may be fine on the tundra or in a barn in northern Michigan, but it can turn a two-bedroom Detroit condominium into a circus of hair balls.

Shedders and nonshedders come in all sizes:

	Shedders	*Nonshedders*
Small breeds	Miniature dachshund Chihuahua Pug Boston terrier	Yorkshire terrier Pomeranian Pekingese Silky terrier
Medium-sized breeds	Beagle Corgi Basenji Dachshund Spaniel Hound	Lhasa apso Bedlington terrier Cairn terrier Scottish terrier Bishon Frise Poodle
Large breeds	Husky Malamute Retriever Setter Pointer	Old English sheepdog Briard Airedale Standard poodle Afghan

Rare Colors

Rare or unusual colors in dogs attract many people. The appearance of a harlequin Great Dane, a blue merle collie, blue Doberman, or white German shepherd will invariably attract more attention than the normal-colored version of the same breed. But if you see such dogs and catch yourself thinking, *Wow, isn't that color unusual,* be sure to ask yourself, *I wonder why?* In many cases, unusual colors are rare because they are not particularly healthy. The blue merle (dark-spotted) collie, for example, is much more susceptible to certain blood diseases than the more common bicolored or tricolored collies. And the offspring of two blue merles tend to be so abnormal that such breeding is strongly discouraged. Odd colors often reflect biological weaknesses that would spell death in the wild. So if you choose a rare lavender-ticked coonhound that was the only one in the litter to survive, thanks to extensive veterinary care, be prepared to spend most of your free time at the vet's with your dog. Mother Nature is giving you some strong hints about this dog's ability to make it on its own. If you have the time to spend fulfilling what may turn out to be very special needs, and if you enjoy the resultant extra fussing and care, such a dog may be ideal for you. But if your life-style requires a low-maintenance dog, stick with standard proven colors.

Breed	*Problem color(s)*
Great Dane	Harlequin, merle, blue
Collie	Blue merle
Doberman	Blue
German Shepherd	White

Purebreds vs. Mongrels

This issue sparks intense debate between pure- and mixed-breed owners. If the debaters were talking about people instead of dogs, we'd think them hopeless bigots. While we can be pretty sure what a purebred pup will look like when it grows up, mongrels often turn out to be canine surprise packages. On the other hand, mongrels often avoid negative characteristics that accompany heavy inbreeding among purebreds.

Surprisingly, the good old reliable mutt isn't as common as it used to be. Purebreds have become so popular that most mongrels are actually half-breeds: half-sheltie–half-beagle, half-poodle–half-cocker. Many times such mixes display less vigor than either parent. For example, conscientious Labrador retriever and German shepherd owners always evaluate their pets' hips for signs of hip disease before breeding; but that doesn't happen when the Schwartzes' shepherd jumps the fence to impregnate the Lewises' Lab. The Lewises couldn't care less about good hip conformation in the resulting mixed-breed pups; people insensitive enough to let their dogs run loose to breed indiscriminately don't care either. Consequently, there can be even more hip problems in such "mongrel" offspring than in the purebreds. Similarly, poodle owners invariably understand the importance of grooming, whereas most poodle mixes resemble walking floor mops. Who bothers grooming a mongrel?

If a particular type of dog appeals to you, go to a pet store or library for books about that breed, but also ask your vet about it. Entire veterinary texts have been devoted to lists of genetic defects and medical problems classified by breed. If you like the easygoing nature of scent hounds such as redbones and Plott hounds, by all means consider one; but don't forget their peculiar and often pungent body odor, which may blow away on the breeze in a North Carolina backyard but will totally overpower a tiny apartment in downtown Philadelphia. The drooly greeting of the more jowly breeds such as Saint Bernards and Great Pyrenees may suit a summer camp environment in northern California but repulse the clientele of the psychologist who works at home in Boston.

Try to match your needs to the characteristics of a particular breed. If you must save for months to buy a particular purebred pup, can you afford the necessary veterinary care, quality diet, and grooming needed to keep that pup healthy? If your favorite breed requires special grooming, are you willing to do it regularly or have it done professionally? Why do you want a purebred dog? Looks? Prestige? Although these are valid reasons, keep in mind that if how you look with the dog at your side means more to you than how the dog itself looks, you're thinking about your prestige, not your dog's. A brown-and-white springer spaniel that is 75 percent white won't be as valuable as the more highly prized 25 percent white standard of show dogs, but it will probably make just as good a family pet, maybe even better if the family prefers a whiter dog.

Life-style	Breed types to avoid
Active, outdoor, erratic	Those that require much grooming—Lhasa, Afghans, Yorkshire terriers
Active, boisterous family	Miniature or toy breeds— easily stepped on Giant breeds—get in the way, knock small children over, harder to control
Hobbies or work involving strong odors, dust, irritants	Brachycephalics (Boston terrier, pug, bulldog, boxer)
Metropolitan environment with much traffic, visual distraction	Sight hounds (greyhound, whippet, Borzoi) and those with strong following reflex that tend to chase cars, moving objects readily
Allergic household member	Heavy shedders, primitive northern breeds (huskies, Samoyeds, Malamutes)

Life-style	Breed types to avoid
Often away from home	Working breeds that need a lot of interaction, such as retrievers, setters, shepherds, Dobermans
Erratic life-style requiring maintenance-free dog	Rare colors, breeds, or exotic coats
Household has other dogs	Pit bulls or breeds bred to fight other dogs

Ask the Person Who Owns One

All the dog books in the world can't replace open dialogue with owners, breeders, handlers, and veterinarians familiar with the breed you're considering. Even though you may not care about pedigree, pay attention to where the "good" and "bad" dogs are coming from. Although golden retrievers in southern New Hampshire may be gentle dogs, those in Sarver, Pennsylvania, may be more aggressive. A friend of mine in Massachusetts owns a bird dog with the most delightful nature, while that same breed in my area can be obnoxious and susceptible to all kinds of behavioral and medical problems.

Such variations within breeds usually result from indiscriminate breeding. For example, golden retrievers are one of several breeds susceptible to hereditary hip problems. Although kennels and professional breeders look for such faults and eliminate individuals possessing them from breeding programs, that doesn't cross the minds of two coworkers at an automotive plant in Detroit who get their male and female littermates at the same time; because their dogs have grown into perfect pets, they want to breed them. If their friends and neighbors also admire the dogs' personalities, the co-workers can conceivably breed these dogs four or more times before either dog displays any hip problems. By that time, the owners have produced as many as forty pups likely to succumb to the same problem as they get older; and some of these offspring may have been bred themselves before their problems appear.

When Dean Jameson bought Daphne, the pup's mother barked and jumped at the door threateningly. The father stood chained outdoors, and the breeder told Dean he couldn't examine him because the pups had made him very aggressive. When Dean began having severe problems with Daphne, at first he thought it was because he was gone so much. However, when he approached other Gordon setter owners in his area, he soon discovered that Daphne's parents tended to produce highly excitable pups that were prone to skin and behavioral problems. Those who were pleased with their Gordons had purchased them from two local women whose dogs enjoyed a reputation for producing easygoing offspring with few medical problems. Live and learn.

Although it would be nice to be able to say that appearance and/or behavior do derive strictly from heredity, a breeder's philosophy and method of training will influence a dog's temperament as much as genes affect eye color. If those beautiful, well-trained, healthy parents result from a full-time training program and special diets, but you're a minimum-wage clerk in a supermarket working sixty-hour weeks, your pup may not turn out like its parents. Save yourself grief by asking owners and breeders many questions about your chosen breed's needs, and relate those needs to your own life-style. If the breeder answers vaguely or not at all, avoid buying his or her pup. Good breeders want their pups to succeed in good homes more than they want to simply sell a dog. Ask for names of those who've bought pups from the breeder in the past.

Learning to Spot Less Desirable Traits

In the paragraphs ahead, we'll concentrate on the less desirable traits of the major groups of dog breeds. It isn't that I dislike or don't recommend these animals (they include some of my best friends and patients), but most books on specific breeds are written by people who love that particular breed. Consequently, they may overlook or minimize the negative. Although these books contain a lot of useful information, we prospective or existing weekend dog owners need to know more about the problems associated with certain breeds or breed types. Don't think these problems can't occur in mixed-breed dogs. A mongrel's composite ancestors affect its behavior and health just as much as a purebred's registered parents.

Mouthy Breeds

Mouthiness refers to an animal's willingness to use its mouth. Many bird dogs exhibit strong mouthiness because they have been bred to retrieve birds. However, mouthiness can vary a great deal from the velvet mouths of the bird dogs (which allow them to retrieve birds without damaging the feathers) to the hard mouths of German shepherds and Dobermans, which have been bred to clamp their jaws tightly. About halfway between the two extremes we find the nippers, such as sheepdogs, shelties, and collies, which are bred to herd cattle or sheep, encouraging them to move with sharp little bites. In the weekend dog, such mouthiness may manifest itself in strange ways. Bored setters that would never consider clamping tightly on a bird may chew up a rug when left alone.

Mouthy Breeds

Soft-mouthed	Hard-mouthed	Herders
Golden retrievers	Dobermans German shepherds	Collies Border collies
Labrador retrievers		Shelties
Setters		Old English
Spaniels		sheepdogs

Long and Short Noses

The endearing, almost infantile expression of the short-nosed (brachycephalic) breeds such as Boston terriers, English bulldogs, pugs, and Pekingese attract many owners. However, anatomical changes associated with this look can create problems. As the nose gets pushed in, the eyes bulge out. Unfortunately, everything else tends to remain the same size: the same amount of skin, the same length of soft palate, and the same forty-two adult teeth crammed into half the space normally available. Compare the nose length of a twenty-pound beagle with that of a similar-weight Boston and you'll wonder how all the beagles' mouthparts could possibly fit into the Boston's head.

What are the consequences of such breeding? Because their eyes bulge, short-snouted dogs are prone to many eye problems if for no other reason than that so much eye is exposed to irritants. Often the tear-draining mechanism does not work properly and tears spill over onto the skin folds around the eyes and muzzle, causing skin infections. A similar condition may arise from saliva in the folds around the mouth. These breeds often have abnormally small nostrils, distorted nasal passages, and a long, soft palate that may even periodically block the windpipe, causing spasms of snorting and coughing. Structural abnormalities also make short-nosed breeds much more susceptible to upper respiratory problems. Until the advent of gas anesthesia in veterinary medicine, these dogs were risky to anesthetize because the peculiarities of the animal's own anatomy could block its airway. Even with modern techniques, such breeds still require much closer monitoring.

The opposite of the brachycephalics are breeds such as collies that have long, narrow noses. These breeds have the same forty-two adult teeth as the beagle and the Boston, but in a much longer jaw. They also have more deeply set eyes. In fact, because of the length and narrowness of the nose, there is often insufficient room for the eyes to develop normally. Consequently, these breeds are more likely to have problems seeing and some eventually may become blind. Unlike the short-nosed breeds whose eye problems are caused by infection, the long-nosed dog's eye defects are caused by the malformation of the eye itself.

So if you spend a lot of time sanding and refinishing antiques, your environment may not suit a pollution-sensitive brachycephalic, and if you live in a neighborhood with a lot of fast traffic where good vision is critical, beware of the long, narrow nosed breeds. Although conscientious breeders of both types of dogs are working hard to reduce these negative qualities, it is difficult to eliminate them without eliminating the snout structure that caused them to begin with. After all, the appearance of the snout attracts some owners to pugs and others to collies.

Big Surprises in Small Packages

Client Bob Richards went through hell with an eighty-pound weekend Malamute that finally chased one car too many. "I finally found the perfect weekend dog," he told me in a supermarket a few months later, "a rat." Bob went on to tell me he was marrying another client of mine, a woman whose long-haired Chihuahua I'd spayed years ago. Could big, gruff, burly Bob, who had lived in the woods with his rough-and-tumble male Malamute, find happiness in the same household with a long-haired, spayed female Chihuahua? He could and did.

"I can't believe it," Bob said later. "I love that little rat. Even when she makes a mistake, it's so little I hardly notice, not like cleaning up after that moose I used to have." Although Bob would still love to have a big dog, a little one fits more snugly into his weekend life-style. He likes dogs, not just big dogs, and can now accept and enjoy what he would have considered a "sissy" breed two years ago.

However, small size did not evolve without sacrifice. Such breeds tend to have more than their share of eye, stifle (knee), and heart problems, as well as epileptic seizures. If owners equate size with stamina, they're likely to assume smaller dogs are quite frail. This isn't always true, but a four-pound Yorkshire terrier's cough does sound more serious than a forty-pound mongrel's. And it is a fact that tiny dogs don't have much weight or size to sustain them when they become ill and stop eating and drinking.

Small breeds are also more likely to get stepped on or injure themselves jumping from their owner's arms. This may seem obvious, yet a lot of people aren't prepared for it. Thirty-pound dogs enjoy less lap time and are less likely to be taught to jump up. Because dogs that jump into their owners' arms eventually want to jump down, accidents will happen. The doorbell rings or your lapdog sees another dog through the window and leaps from your arms, falls, and breaks a leg. This can be a traumatic experience for weekend dog owners who must at least temporarily change their life-styles to accommodate the injury (see Chapter 12).

Owner beliefs about smaller dogs seem to be more tenacious and emotional than those associated with other breeds. People are more likely to stereotype them as "yappy," "nippy," "fussy eaters," "impossible to housebreak," and "high-strung." Even the most ardent small dog owner uses such terms. However, I have encountered the full range of excitability in *all* breeds. For example, in my area black Labradors tend to be much more exuberant and excitable than Chihuahuas. Although I do see some very bouncy poodles, the majority tend to be pretty low-keyed.

It's best to avoid attributing *behavioral* qualities to a particular breed, because such qualities usually depend on training or lack of it rather than on any genetic tendencies. If Mrs. Treno's toy poodle isn't housebroken and eats only steak, that's probably not because it's a toy poodle, but because the owner has certain beliefs about housebreaking and dog food. But because many people believe such behavior is natural for toy poodles, Mrs. Treno can keep her untrained fussy eater without suffering much negative public opinion. If she owned an unhousebroken, steak-eating Great Dane, she would probably receive a lot of criticism.

White Elephants

The giant breeds pose their own special problems. Not only are they more prone to hip problems and bone cancers, they have more trouble adjusting to inconsistent weekend schedules. If the Rossmans' cocker pulls some leg muscles after a weekend of unaccustomed exercise and doesn't want to go down the eight steps to the backyard to relieve herself, Bruce Rossman can easily carry the dog up and down the stairs. But what can their neighbor Carol Pingatelli do with her 175-pound Saint Bernard when it suffers similar symptoms?

Some large-breed problems are so obvious, we tend to overlook them. For example, everything costs more with a big dog. They eat more, they outgrow more collars, and they need bigger, stronger fences, kennels, or runs to confine them. While the Rossmans' spaniel chews nervously on the rug in the back hall during a thunderstorm, the Pingatellis' Saint Bernard rips apart a living room window trying to escape.

All sorts of dogs may suffer the same treatable illnesses, which veterinarians almost always medicate according to weight. Consider a common antibiotic with a recommended dosage of 10 milligrams per pound of body weight: the drug comes in 250-milligram tablets, each costing ten cents, and should be given three times daily for one week. Now compare the prescription for the Rossmans' spaniel and the Pingatellis' Saint Bernard:

	Weight	Number of pills	Cost
Spaniel	25 lbs.	21	$ 2.10
Saint Bernard	175 lbs.	147	$14.70

Not only does it cost seven times more to medicate the larger dog, it also costs more to feed it, groom it, or travel with it. If you're a potential weekend dog owner on a limited budget, such costs could affect your weekend dog selection.

The Secondhand Dog

All of us have seen advertisements in our local papers that read: "Free Dog. Four-year-old mixed breed needs happy home and room to run." Like free lunches, free dogs don't exist. Although the ad implies you're getting a housebroken, well-behaved pet, in today's society that seldom happens. Many older dogs find their way into the want ads or humane societies because they have behavioral problems, often resulting from a weekend life-style. Consequently, you may wind up owning a dog with the very problems you thought you'd avoid by getting an adult.

Sure, secondhand treasures abound, but always ask one question before you adopt any older dog: *Why is this dog being given up?* Because the bond between a well-behaved, healthy dog and its owner tends to be a strong one, people who share such a bond rarely find themselves in positions where they can't keep their pets. They'd never consider separation. On the other hand, a large number of dog owners seek new homes for their dogs because the dogs just didn't work out. Dogs don't work out for reasons ranging from the new baby's allergies to the dog's aggressive behavior toward the postman. In the former case, a childless couple might be getting a perfect secondhand dog, whereas they might end up paying dearly for the latter. Beware of ads that sound too good to be true. They usually are. Be open and honest with the current owner about your needs and expectations.

If you sense any owner hesitancy or reluctance to answer your questions, think twice about taking the dog, or arrange to take it for a *specific* trial period. Trial periods let you test the dog in your own environment, but they also set you up emotionally. Many softhearted people get snookered in during a trial period by those big brown eyes or the previous owner's hints about putting the dog to sleep if a new owner can't be found. Our relationships with our dogs are already sufficiently complicated by guilt; selecting a dog because someone tries to lay a guilt trip on you only leads to more misery.

Smart Dogs in Dull Surroundings

Often we are drawn to a particular breed or a particular dog because it's intelligent; but intelligence in dogs, like people, can be a matter of opinion. Not all dumb blondes are dumb, and some great minds have trouble tying their shoelaces. Most common definitions of an intelligent dog include a willingness to learn, a certain spontaneity, and a smart expression or look. Regardless of the specific definition, all dog lovers recognize and demand some form of it in their dogs.

Many potential weekend dog owners are attracted to working dogs such as golden and Labrador retrievers, English and Irish setters, or Irish water or springer spaniels because these dogs are known for intelligence. In addition to being important to hunters, their "soft mouth" manifests itself as gentleness in a household pet. That's the good news. The bad news is that such dogs were bred to work, to *use* all that intelligence and mouthiness—not to sit alone in a three-bedroom split level in West Palm Beach eight hours a day, five days a week. In such a setting their intelligence may lead to destructive behavior.

Many other kinds of dogs originally were bred to do specific chores. Borzois, poodles, Afghans, greyhounds, beagles, coonhounds, Plott hounds, pointers, Newfoundlands, corgis, dachshunds, and fox terriers, for example, were all originally bred for one form of hunting or another. Although not as mouthy as the bird dogs, these breeds are nonetheless as intelligent and as prone to destructive behavior when bored.

Potential weekend dog owners or current owners with problem dogs can learn a lot by attending field and obedience trials, observing their favorite breeds perform, and then reexamining their homes and life-styles. Your golden retriever, beagle, Gordon setter, collie, sheltie, puli, or poodle has the same breed characteristics and energy as its counterpart in the field or ring; but what outlet does (or will) your dog have for its energy in your home?

Intelligent dogs that get bored do things people regard as destructive: they eat plants, chew rugs, upset the trash, and dig holes. Even if you train the dog not to destroy your home, that energy will still be there, and then the only outlet left for the dog is its own body. Many chronic skin and ear problems result from boredom. A smart dog bred to work feels a little tickle in its ear or on its skin and goes after it harder and longer. Such persistence is great in the field, but can result in a large oozing sore or infected ear in less than a day. We can almost hear our dogs saying, *If I have to be by myself all day and can't chew on the geraniums, then I'll chew on myself.*

In later chapters on training and exercise, we'll see ways to relieve some of this boredom; but nothing can relieve breeding characteristics. The following guidelines will help you select the right weekend dog for you.

- Make a list of those qualities you want and need in your dog.
- Trust your intuition, especially regarding the wrong dog for you.
- Determine how much time you can spend with your dog.
- Estimate how much you can afford to spend on a dog. This should include not only purchase price, but also upkeep, grooming, licensing, neutering, changes required to dog-proof (Chapter 3) your home, etc.
- Learn all you can about the breed(s) you're interested in. Read books on the subject, but also talk to owners of similar dogs, veterinarians, and kennel people. Tell them about your life-style. Find out what's wrong with your potential breed choice as well as what's right with it.
- If your potential dog has certain limitations, either physical or behavioral, evaluate them in terms of your life-style.
- When considering an adult dog, always find out why it's being sold or given away.

CHAPTER 3

Building a Workable Weekend Philosophy

"**S**ay, isn't that a new '83 Shepherd you're walking?"
"Yeah, my '79 Retriever wasn't doing so hot so I traded her in."

Owning a dog isn't like owning a car. Cars are things. Dogs, though not people, aren't things either. If a car breaks down, we can hire someone to fix it or trade it in. If our relationship with our dog breaks down, it takes a lot more than a trip to the vet or a change in diet to set it right. Building a workable relationship with a weekend dog demands a special approach, a new philosophy which, fortunately, both dog and owner can easily develop.

"If It Ain't Broken, Don't Fix It"

Because inconsistency so often characterizes weekend life-styles, weekend dog owners must be adaptable, willing to change their relationships with their pets if necessary. When evaluating your own philosophy, consider the following: in the first place, if your relationship with your dog satisfies you, regardless of what others say, you may not want to change it. As the New Hampshire philosopher says, "If it ain't broke, don't fix it!" And secondly, if the relationship doesn't satisfy you or your dog, perhaps one or both of you should change.

To objectively evaluate your current philosophy, ask yourself the following questions, paying attention not only to your answers, but also to your feelings about your answers. If you don't yet own a dog, imagine yourself with one.

- If your dog disappeared tomorrow, how would you react? Would you feel guilty, upset, or relieved?
- What do your neighbors and friends think about your relationship with your dog? Do their opinions bother you?
- If you could magically change some aspect of your relationship with your dog, what would it be?
- Do you ever do things to your pet that you feel guilty about?
- If you had it to do all over again, would you get *this* dog? Any dog?

Your answers to these questions and your feelings about them should quickly reveal how you view your relationship with your dog.

Both People and Dogs Can Change

Let's look at two springer spaniels, twelve-week-old littermates, exhibiting normal, exuberant puppy jumping behavior, to see how two different people react to it. Why do puppies jump up on people? Like people, they want to establish eye contact, and the surest way for a ten-pound pup to establish eye contact with an adult human is to leap as high as possible. This jumping, usually accompanied with much tail-wagging and sometimes even barking and whining, is the dog's way of saying, *Welcome home! Where've you been all day? Boy, am I glad to see you!* In Chapter 7 we'll discuss specific ways to deal with this behavior, but for now, let's concentrate on people's reaction to it.

Sue Jacobs, a fashion consultant, has had her springer, Willow, for a little over a month, and it's been a disaster. She wants an affectionate pet, but the wild jumping and carrying-on each evening are ruining her feelings about the pup. It's also ruining her clothes. Sue must wear expensive dresses and suits to work, and she dreads coming home each evening to face the exuberant Willow. Willow has already ruined six pairs of panty hose, two designer dresses, and a silk blouse.

Cathy Clay bought Lilly, Willow's littermate, to keep her semi-invalid father company while Cathy's at work. Nothing delights the elderly Mr. Clay more than watching Lilly bounce, and he laughs and praises her whenever she jumps into his arms. Their relationship pleases Cathy, who hasn't seen her father so happy in months.

Both pups are exhibiting the same behavior, yet Sue defines it as wrong, while Cathy thinks it's right. Which is it? Obviously, it depends on one's point of view. When Willow ruins Sue's skirt, Sue cannot help being angry at the pup. And when she's angry at Willow, Sue starts to wonder why she ever got a dog in the first place. *Is there something wrong with me?* she wonders. *Am I too strict, too lax, or not home enough?* The more Sue thinks about it, the guiltier she feels. And without a doubt, guilt is the most damaging, unproductive emotion a weekend dog owner can suffer. Before Sue sinks into a quagmire of guilt, she may want to consider her four possible choices:

1. Continue the current guilt-producing situation with no change.
2. Let Willow continue the behavior, but change the way she feels about it (i.e., not let it bother her when the pup ruins her clothes).
3. Get rid of the pup.
4. Align Willow's behavior with her beliefs (i.e., train the pup, or have the pup trained not to jump).

The correct choice depends solely on Sue's experience and beliefs. Because she wants to keep Willow and still wear nice clothing, Sue opts for number 4 and enrolls Willow in puppy obedience classes. Although many of you may agree with Sue's choice, the other options could be correct in certain circumstances.

If we had asked Cathy and her father which choice they would make, they would undoubtedly have shouted, "Number one! Lilly's behavior is wonderful. We wouldn't change her for the world." Not *at this time,* perhaps.

I stress "at this time" because little about our relationships with our dogs is eternal. Relationships and the conditions surrounding them evolve, change, and grow every day. What works today may not work tomorrow. Dogs change. People change. Both grow older. People marry or divorce. We have children, our dogs have puppies. With each change comes a new set of conditions that may make a big difference. Consider what happened with Cathy and Lilly:

When Lilly was five years old, Cathy's father died. About a year later Cathy married an insurance executive who prides himself on his immaculate appearance. He and Cathy constantly argue over Lilly's jumping behavior. Now how does Cathy feel about it? The same behavior that used to bring such joy now causes profound guilt and unhappiness. Why did she ever allow such behavior in the first place?

Now Cathy finds herself facing the same four possibilities that confronted Sue Jacobs. Instead of dwelling on what she might have done differently in the past, she should consider her options now. In Cathy's case, number 3, getting rid of the dog, makes the most sense because her husband doesn't like the dog anyway and her cousin wants to give Lilly a good home in the country.

It Doesn't Hurt to Laugh

Besides being willing to change beliefs and adapt to changing circumstances, no trait helps the weekend dog owner more than a sense of humor. I remember coming home from work one day to discover that my dog, Dufie, had hollowed out a whole layer cake I had absentmindedly left on the kitchen counter. The floor was covered with sticky crumbs, and Dufie's stomach rumbled like a volcano about to erupt. I knew it was useless to discipline Dufie for something he had done hours before. I considered my alternatives:

1. Scream at the dog anyhow.
2. Ignore the dog and angrily clean up the mess.
3. Feel guilty because my own negligence had caused my dog great discomfort.
4. Laugh.

I laughed. This doesn't mean that I didn't care about Dufie's suffering or that I continue to leave tempting foods on the counter. But it does mean I've learned that an atmosphere of happiness not only produces quicker results, but also longer-lasting results. Dogs pick up subtle cues from people and vice versa. Dufie's physical and emotional ailments, like my own, seem to decline in direct proportion to the amount of interest others show in them. Learn to evaluate the situation quickly and objectively. If it's too late to do anything but clean up, then clean up cheerfully. Anger not only confuses your dog, it doesn't solve the problem. Had I yelled at Dufie, I'm sure I would have gotten that confused look which I now translate as, *Wow, she's really in a foul mood today! Think I'll get out of her way, maybe go lie down under the bed. My stomach hurts.*

Dufie would undoubtedly recognize that I was angry, but have no idea why. Cleaning up isn't my idea of fun, but being mad at myself and my dog while cleaning up after him isn't any more fun. A business-as-usual or, better, love-as-usual attitude after some perceived transgression helps solve the problem more effectively. This doesn't mean that weekend dog owners should take serious medical or behavioral problems lightly; but it does mean that weekend dog owners, like all dog owners, should strive to make their relationships with their dogs fun.

Is Your Castle
Your Dog's Home, Too?

Many times people say they like dogs who know their place. For some people, the dog's place is in a kennel in the farthest corner of the backyard. For others, it's between satin sheets in the master bedroom. Developing an awareness of the value you attach to your surroundings in relationship to your pet is a great help to existing or potential weekend dog owners. If you are fond of delicate Dresden figurines or take great pride in your garden of prize-winning tea roses, but want a dog anyway, you may have to rearrange your environment or alter your feelings about it. No dog, no matter how well trained, is ever completely trustworthy in either house or yard. However, even if you lack the necessary time to teach your dog not to sleep on the furniture, leave the yard, bark, chew, dig, or display other problem-creating behavior in your absence, you can always try dog-proofing.

Dog-proofing refers to those changes weekend dog owners make in their surroundings to circumvent certain negative behavior. Don't look at it as building a prison for the dog or for your possessions; be creative and flexible. Some common dog-proofing measures include:

- Chain link or stockade fencing. Imagine the freedom your dog can enjoy within the confines of a fence. Can you design a fence that enhances your property?
- Sturdy outdoor kennels or runs. Why not include a dog palace or an attractive playground (see Chapter 10).
- Indoor kennels. Would your dog enjoy its own special den where it can get away for some peace and quiet?
- Barricades to prevent illicit grazing or napping on furniture in the owner's absence. Who cares if you up-end your dining room chairs on the new sofa while you're out?
- Locks or some other type of security on kitchen cabinets and other accessible food sources. (These can benefit the children, too.)

Let's examine a few situations where the owner's sense of place and dog-proofing play a major role in the weekend dog–owner relationship.

Tim Collins, a sound engineer for a San Francisco rock group, loves his tiny apartment in a renovated townhouse. His dog, Motown, does too—as long as Tim's there. But as soon as Tim leaves for work. Motown starts barking . . . and keeps barking. It got so bad, the neighbors complained and Tim's landlord told him to either get rid of the dog or move. Because Tim likes both his dog and his home, he spent two weekends building a comfortable soundproof area where Motown can bark freely.

Free-lance photographer Dorie Litman's 140-pound Newfoundland, Kodak, unleashes spine-chilling howls whenever Dorie leaves him alone. Like Motown, Kodak is a social dog that likes to be with other dogs or people and loudly voices his frustration when left alone. Because Dorie never really liked apartment living, she responded to her landlord's get-rid-of-the-dog-or-move ultimatum by packing up and moving to a fifty-acre farm where Kodak can howl at will.

Sherman Leaward collects antique bottles, which he neatly arranges by color and manufacturer on nearly every windowsill in his home. His one and only dog, an exuberant setter, broke over a thousand dollars' worth of glassware trying to get at a squirrel through a window; Sherman got rid of the dog immediately and has not allowed an animal into his house since.

In all three cases, the owner chose to alter his or her surroundings rather than the dog's behavior. Both Tim and Sherman have a very strong sense of place, but Tim's sense of place includes a dog, even if it means depriving himself of living space in his cramped quarters, while Sherman's does not. For Dorie, where she lives matters less than living hassle-free with Kodak. All three discovered that environmental changes, including getting rid of the dog, offer the fastest solution to many common weekend dog problems. Such solutions may be expensive and may even seem bizarre and unfeeling, but they can quickly elliminate a lot of problems. Whether or not owners can carry out specific environmental changes depends on which they prize most: their dogs or their sense of place.

Feeling Good
About Your Philosophy

The final, but by no means least important characteristic of a successful weekend dog owner is confidence. *Do I feel good about the quality of my dog's life? Do I feel good about the quality of my life in relationship to my dog's?*

Abstract questions? Not really. The following quiz will help you determine how confident you are regarding your relationship with your dog.

1. You are restraining your dog in the middle of a boisterous group of youngsters when the dog suddenly slips out of his collar and takes off. Do you:

    a. Lose your temper and scream at the dog, brandishing its collar and leash like a whip?
    b. Shake your head sadly and go home to wait for the dog officer's call?
    c. Drop quickly to your knees, making broad welcoming gestures with your arms to lure it back?

2. You and your dog have been having a great time every Monday evening for the past two years watching football on TV and sharing a bowl of popcorn. Your mother comes over one Monday and tells you you're going to kill the dog with that kind of food. The dog has never been sick a day in its life. Do you:

    a. Stop watching TV and eating popcorn, and do something else with your dog?
    b. Put the dog outside while you watch TV?
    c. Continue with the Monday night ritual?

3. Every day when you come home from work, you clean up soiled papers and take the dining room chairs off the table. A friend accompanies you one day and shakes her head, saying, "You're out of your mind going through all that for a dog!" Do you:

    a. Make excuses for yourself and your dog?
    b. Get angry and tell your friend to mind her own business?
    c. Ignore her comments and change the subject?

I can imagine situations where any of these answers might make sense, although in each case I think *c* shows more owner confidence. Let's look at an example:

Ian and Katy Simons decide to celebrate their twenty-five years in business together by having a cocktail party for all their friends and business acquaintances. Halfway through the party their dog, Hunter, saunters through the back door reeking of skunk. The party climaxes with several of the guests wrestling the reluctant mastiff into the tub to deodorize him.

"Best party we ever had!" beams Ian, stroking the still wet mastiff two hours later.

Such an incident could have been a nightmare, but Ian and Katy's genuine affection for their dog and their confidence in that relationship carries them through easily.

I certainly hope your dog never disrupts your life the way the Simons's mastiff did. However, I can't overemphasize the importance of confidence when encountering:

- A favorite lamp or vase smashed to bits on the living room floor.
- A large, damp, yellow stain on the new oriental rug.
- An irate meter reader with a tear in his or her trousers.
- A gaping hole in your new car's upholstery.
- Dog vomit on the bed.
- A neighbor's dead cat or uprooted prize peonies lying next to your dog on your front porch.

If we do not have a workable philosophy to guide our relationship with our dogs, any of these events can be catastrophic. If we have no philosophy, then we must begin from scratch with each event. We must react, then act. This takes time, and weekend dog owners don't usually have much time because we're so busy cramming our living into evenings and weekends. And rather than spend that valuable time training our dogs, we often scream at them or hit them instead. Screaming or hitting rarely changes

anything, although it can certainly make us feel more
guilty. And when guilt strikes, we just add one more problem to the original one. Even if we do have a great deal of
free time, we'd rather spend it feeling good about ourselves and our dogs.

Before you rush outside to pound your dog for barking
again, or before you run next door to claim one of those
adorable little cocker pups for your own, quickly review
those qualities needed to maintain a good relationship
with a dog these days:

- A *willingness to change one's philosophy.* For the existing owner this may mean changing beliefs or trying
  different training techniques. For the potential weekend dog owner, it may mean many environmental and
  personal changes.
- An *ability to adapt to new circumstances and behav-*
  iors. Relationships with dogs evolve. It is a rare dog or
  person who can establish certain physical or behavioral patterns that never change.
- A *sense of humor.* Being able to approach even the
  worst experience with laughter cuts through the negative emotions to reveal the lesson and makes weekend dog ownership more enjoyable for both you and
  your dog.
- An *awareness of the values you attach to your envi-*
  ronment. If you invest a lot of meaning or emotion in
  objects that might get in a growing pup's or dog's way,
  your relationship with your pet will surely suffer unless you train your dog properly or dog-proof your
  property.
- *Confidence.* If you firmly believe that the dog and philosophy you have are right for you, you can save yourself and your dog a lot of problems in the future.

CHAPTER 4

Getting Off to a Good Start

O ver the mantel in his den, John Brown displays numerous trophies he and his hunting dog have won at field trials all over the country. Yet the dog has never been inside John's house.

Adele Metzger is unemployed, but hardly nonworking. Since her children have grown, she devotes almost thirty hours a week to various community service projects as well as belonging to a tournament bridge club. Her Pomeranian, Trinket, has the best of everything: gourmet food, her own special bed next to Adele's. Adele doesn't even expect the dog to relieve herself outdoors if the weather's bad. Because it seems the dog has everything, Adele finds it increasingly difficult to reconcile Trinket's destructive behavior in her absence as well as her own guilty feelings about leaving the dog alone so much.

Karen Bauer got Rudyard, a four-year-old terrier mix, from the humane society because she doesn't have time to train a pup while she's working. About the only command the dog seems to know is "Seek and destroy."

In this and the next three chapters we'll examine those aspects of training most valuable to the weekend owner. First we'll look at basic training attitudes and the tools that best utilize these attitudes. Then we'll learn how to teach a weekend pup the basics, including a separate chapter on housebreaking. We'll complete our discussion of training with advice on correcting bad habits in older dogs that we or a previous owner or life-style may have caused.

What Is a Well-trained Dog?

Retired army colonel Charlie Porter walks his German shepherd up and down the street twice daily without a leash. The dog immediately sits quietly whenever Charlie stops. It ignores other dogs and distractions. Together Charlie and the dog seem to function as a unit.

"Isn't that dog great!" exclaims Karen Bauer to her housemate as they unload groceries from the car after a long day at work. They listen to their dog, Rudyard, frantically barking at the shepherd, knowing he's perched on the back of the couch, his wet nose and tongue smearing the picture window.

Every dog owner wants a well-trained dog, but what does that mean? There are surely as many definitions of a well-trained dog as there are dog owners. John Brown insists that a well-trained dog means a totally disciplined field dog, a dog with plenty of stamina that can live year-round in a kennel with little attention yet perform superbly whenever commanded. On the other hand, Adele Metzger says Trinket became well trained the instant she learned to wet on newspapers. And, according to Adele,

Trinket became *exceptionally* well trained when she learned to eat table food from her owner's spoon. For most of us, though, the definition of a well-trained dog lies somewhere between these two extremes.

Regardless of your position, you've probably adopted it because of your beliefs and life-style. Pressed for time, many weekend dog owners abandon classic notions that a well-trained dog is totally housebroken and always responds to the commands come, sit, and stay. We weekend dog owners will gladly settle for a seldom destructive, almost housebroken dog that more or less hangs around the house. Does this mean we contemporary dog owners have lowered our standards? Not really. Many of us have just become more realistic because we know we don't have the time to create the ideal well-trained dog we remember from our childhood.

Nevertheless, we can adopt specific time-saving techniques that will enable us to enjoy our pets without the constant fear of ruined property and angry neighbors. As you might expect, it all starts with beliefs.

How We Think Our Dogs Think

People tend to project their own beliefs into the heads of their dogs. If you hold the Independent view which defines dogs as a totally separate species, you probably attribute a certain amount of wild dog or wolf-type thinking to them. People holding this view often approach dog training as an interspecies power struggle wherein they strive to prove their superiority over the dog. Because supporters of this approach believe humans have nothing in common with the dog species, they seldom attempt interspecies communication, but see dogs as aliens on which they must impose their own wishes. Such a grim-faced approach does not permit learning to be fun for the dog or the owner, but sees it as a battle of wills from beginning

to end. If such owners fail to create a well-trained dog by
their own standards, they feel they've failed. As with all
other aspects of weekend dog ownership, feelings of failure cause guilt, which only makes things worse. Let's
watch the Independent belief in action.

Marty Shuman has had Curry, a Samoyed mix, since the
dog was a pup. At age two, Curry chews furniture legs into
toothpicks whenever Marty leaves her alone. From the beginning, Marty has used rolled-up newspaper and even his
belt to discipline the dog. Although Curry always cowers
when beaten, she continues chewing because she doesn't
connect the punishment with the crime committed hours
before. Once Marty beat her so hard he had to leave the
house in a storm of guilty rage, pausing only long enough
to shake his fist at the confused Curry and scream, "No stupid dog's going to get the best of me!" Because Curry has
ruined every piece of Marty's furniture, he's embarrassed
to invite friends to his home. "I'm a top-notch accountant,"
he complains. "Why the hell can't I train a stupid dog?"

Those who adhere to the Dependent Species view that
dogs are fuzzy subhumans often find themselves just as
frustrated as Marty Shuman. While the Martys of this world
tend to practice interspecies antagonism, those who view
their dogs as backward children can practically love them
to death, even though they take the dog's failure to learn
as a personal condemnation. Whereas those with the Independent view will not give a dog credit for any communication ability, proponents of the Dependent view give
them too much. If Trinket wets on the rug when Adele
Metzger leaves her alone, Adele shakes her head sadly.
"Trinket just hates it when I play bridge with Louise
Thompson. Louise has a horrible old cat and I just know
poor Trinket smells him on my skirt and is insanely jealous. She wets to punish me." Adele has similar excuses for
Trinket's misbehavior when she attends planning board or
hospital auxillary meetings or choir practice or goes shopping with a friend.

How about the Bonded view that sits somewhere between the other two? Bonded advocates believe dogs and people can communicate, but as dogs and people. As with any kind of communication between individuals with different ideas, beliefs, or languages, we must learn to understand each other. Perhaps the main characteristic of those holding the Bonded view is their eagerness to know how their dogs think without projecting their own thoughts on them. Let's drop in on Karen Bauer and her weekend dog, Rudyard.

Karen took Rudyard from the local animal shelter two weeks ago and from the beginning the two-year-old terrier mix messed in the house. Today it happened again. After cleaning up the mess, Karen sits down next to her pet and strokes the wirey coat gently. "You know, Rudy, this has to stop. Sometimes I get so mad at you I could just pound the daylights out of you. Why don't you make messes while I'm home so I can train you? Is that it? You mess because I'm not home? You don't like being alone?"

Perhaps this doesn't sound like particularly meaningful communication, but Karen is not only articulating her needs and frustrations but also attempting to understand Rudy. She does not see herself involved in a power struggle with the dog, nor does she respond to him as she would to a child. Her attitude helps create an environment where both owner and dog can work together to solve the problem.

Selecting the Right Training Method for You and Your Dog

Many excellent training books describe methods weekend dog owners can easily adapt to their special needs. What works or feels right for one trainer may not work or feel right for you. If a particular method does not seem appropriate for you or your dog, try another one. Some people prefer a peppy training session while others prefer a more low-keyed one. If you like the latter, you'll feel uncomfortable with exuberant techniques; if you prefer the former, the slower, more controlled methods will bore you. You may also discover that one method works well for teaching your dog to sit but an opposite approach works better when teaching it to stay.

Above all, you and your dog should be comfortable with the method of discipline recommended by any source because this is one area where consistency is a must. Obviously, different people feel different about the correct way to discipline a dog. In their book *How to Be Your Dog's Best Friend* (Little, Brown and Co., 1978), the Monks of New Skete offer some excellent suggestions on this touchy subject, and I highly recommend it to all weekend dog owners. Nevertheless, keep in mind that any method of discipline must feel natural to you or you won't be able to use it effectively. If some training procedure recommends teaching your dog to sit using a quick snap of its choke collar and giving it a sharp rap on the rump with a rolled newspaper if it resists, and you find such physical actions distasteful, chances are you won't stick with such training very long. Even if you find these techniques acceptable, if you're a 100-pound woman training a 180-pound Newfoundland, you may be physically unable to implement them. By the same token, a 250-pound man must exercise extreme care when physically disciplining a 5-pound poodle.

If small children or an elderly friend or relative will be handling the dog, select a disciplinary technique these people can also use. It does no good if Marty can grab Curry's attention with a quick yank on her choke collar but a seven-year-old nephew is the one trying to control her. Trinket depends so much on Adele Metzger that the slightest sound upsets her. If her owner were to smack the countertop with a ruler to distract her from some misbehavior, or swat her with a rolled-up newspaper, Trinket would recoil in terror, possibly committing additional negative behavior like wetting on the floor. On the other hand, Karen Bauer finds it so hard to control Rudyard when the doorbell rings that only a very loud noise or even a swat will suffice to get his attention.

A *further note:* If you plan to train your dog for show or obedience work, avoid mixing different training methods. The various approaches may produce subtle variations in the dog's response that, although inconsequential to most pet owners, may matter a great deal to a show judge.

Training the Dog for
Its Weekend Life-Style

Many people often get a pup when they're on vacation with the idea that they'll have more time to train it then. Although that's true, you'll enjoy more lasting results if you train your dog for its inevitable weekend life-style from the beginning. Many schoolteachers who get pups in June and train them over the summer get a shock when they go back to school in the fall and their dogs begin misbehaving. No matter how nicely your dog acts when you're home, that's no indication of how it will act when you're not. A weekend dog owner can circumvent a lot of problems involving stay-at-home neighbors by enlisting the neighbors' help in evaluating the dog's behavior in the owner's absence. Often neighbors believe the dog acts the same way when the owner is home and think the owner just chooses to ignore it—and the neighbors' feelings. Simultaneously, the weekend dog may behave perfectly in the owner's presence, causing the owner to wrongly assume that's always the case.

Know Your Training Goal
Before beginning to train your weekend dog, be sure you know what kind of behavior you want. This may seem

obvious, but many times weekend dog owners get so bogged down just keeping the dog nondestructive or quiet, they completely lose sight of their original goals. When Karen Bauer comes to me and wants to know how to stop her dog from digging up the backyard, I first ask, "Why is Rudy tied out in the backyard?" Of course, many weekend owners already know why Karen ties him outdoors: if he were indoors, he'd destroy the house. What Karen really wants is a dog she can trust in the house.

Make Learning Fun for Yourself and Your Dog

If you don't enjoy both teaching and learning yourself, you should probably send your weekend dog to a professional trainer. If you enjoy it to a point, but then find yourself becoming impatient or bored, take a break. Many training books offer specific recommendations about the length of the training session from the dog's point of view, but owners have their needs, too. What if Karen can only tolerate Rudyard's exuberant behavior for ten minutes instead of the half hour recommended by the pet store owner? Maybe it will take Karen longer to train him, but she'll do a much better job if she responds to her own needs as well as her dog's. Make learning fun. If it's not, go back to the beginning, to your beliefs and expectations, and readjust them to reflect your life-style.

Training Tools for the Weekend Dog Owner

Establish Eye Contact with Your Dog

Eye contact facilitates training because it establishes a line of communication between dog and owner. It has been said that the eyes mirror the mind; if this is true, eye contact can teach us a great deal about how people and animals think. Rather than forcing the dog to look at you by holding its head, use sound or motion cues instead. Sometimes just holding your hand level with the dog's nose, then quickly raising it to your face will cause the dog

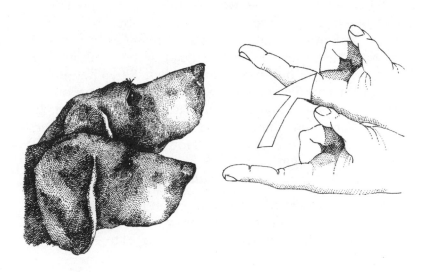

Figure 4–1 Notice how the hand is used to establish eye contact. With your palm and finger turned upward, you are beckoning your dog to look at you. Make sure you don't point at the dog instead; this can be intimidating to shy animals.

to look at you. Suddenly speaking the dog's name or whistling sharply also works well.

Establishing eye contact is important because, unlike people whose vision is more sensitive to detail, dogs tend to respond more readily to motion. The motion of passing cars, other household members, wind, or other animals will easily distract a dog during training. By accustoming the dog to look at you and praising it for doing so, you establish an effective pathway for communication. This also further aids training because some dogs apparently think, *If I don't look at you, I can pretend you're not here.*

Responsive Attention

When we train a dog, we give the dog a stimulus, the dog makes a response, and we reward the proper one. Suppose Karen Bauer sits down to read her paper and Rudyard runs over and lays his head on her arm, making it impossible for her to continue reading. Karen puts down the paper and pets the dog. Soon the terrier tires of the petting and walks away, leaving Karen to resume reading. What's happening here? Karen would probably answer, "I'm petting my dog. Big deal." However, much more has occurred. To begin with, Karen and Rudyard have turned the normal training pattern inside out:

Stimulus: Rudyard sticks his head in Karen's lap.
Response: Karen puts down her paper and pets the dog.
Reward: Rudyard leaves Karen alone to finish her paper.

In other words, the dog is training Karen and by her response, Karen is communicating to him that he doesn't have to do anything but bother her to gain her attention. Is it any wonder that Rudyard and many rowdy pups and dogs subscribe to the following dog logic: *My owner loves me just the way I am and I can teach her/him to pet me anytime I want.*

Such dogs present a frustrating dilemma: can loving owners condemn a dog that only wants love? Poor Rudyard, who spends many hours alone while Karen works, just wants to be loved when she's home. However, if we really understand this subtle shift of power, we see that we are doing our dogs (and our love for them) no favors by inadvertently reinforcing such behavior.

At this point, Dependent-school believers will sigh deeply and accuse Rudyard of trying to punish Karen for leaving him home so much, while those of the Independent school will assume their alien species battle stations and shout, "We'll show him who's boss!" Neither traditional belief will help Karen create a well-trained dog. On the other hand, the Bonded view recognizes Rudy as an intelligent dog that wants to love his owner, and Karen as an intelligent person who wants to love her dog, and asks: *How can I use this knowledge to make both of us happier?* The answer is simple: allow the dog to *earn* the petting, allow it to succeed. If Karen withholds all petting and fondling until Rudyard responds to some command, even if only for a few seconds, she demonstrates that learning is as much an enjoyable part of their relationship as love. She replaces her dog's *I know Karen will love me regardless of what I do, so I don't have to learn anything,* with the more mutually rewarding, *It pleases Karen so much when I do what she asks, it makes me happy, too!*

Now Karen is establishing an active, fulfilling relationship with her dog instead of the original stagnant one based on guilt. Weekend dog owners who tolerate a dominant, demanding pet often do so out of a sense of guilt, not love. And guilt provides the shakiest of all foundations upon which to build a training program or a relationship.

Understand Your Dog's Retention Span

The length of the dog's retention span has been estimated as anything from a few seconds to a few hours. Retention span refers to that period of time during which your dog will associate your reaction to a certain act to the act itself. If Rudy recognizes at 5:15 that Karen is angry at him for chewing up the newspaper at 5:00, then his retention span is at least fifteen minutes.

Although scientific studies do not agree on canine retention span, weekend dog owners should consider thirty to sixty *seconds* a working average. Why so short? Since Karen leaves for work at 7:30 A.M. and gets home at 5:30 P.M., the chances of catching the terrier red-handed are almost nil; so if she tells herself she must be there within thirty to sixty seconds of any negative act, she establishes a workable rule of thumb that eliminates her anger and guilt about not catching Rudyard in the act. This frees Karen to drive to and from work without agonizing, guilt-laden thoughts like: *Oh my God, I left the pot roast uncovered on the stove! Oh, oh, I forgot the plumber was coming today! I hope my roommate took the dog out before he left for class. I hope I get home before my sister arrives, just in case Rudy.* . . .

These may all be legitimate fears, but there's nothing constructive Karen is able to do about them. It is far more beneficial for her to spend the drive home from work thinking about the pleasant things she and Rudy will do *after* she cleans up the mess and takes the dining room chairs off the living room couch.

Denning

An understanding and acceptance of the concept of denning can benefit the weekend dog owner more than all the self-help books on the market. Denning involves placing the dog in a crate or fiber glass kennel big enough to hold it, a blanket, and a favorite toy. This accomplishes two things. First, by limiting the dog's area, we limit the area of potential destruction. Second, denning provides a safe haven for the dog, a secure place which takes the *need* to protect its territory (an extremely strong instinct in dogs) completely out of the animal's control.

Does this idea bother you? Do you feel that denning your dog is cruel and unusual punishment? If so, you have a people problem with a technique that, far from hurting your dog, keeps it safe and happy and nondestructive.

To get your dog into its den, repeat key phrases such as "Kennel up" or "In you go, Rudy" every time you wish to crate your dog. Before long the phrase alone will automatically trigger the desired behavior. It also helps to give the dog a special toy it only gets to have in the den. One client "stores" this toy in the dirty laundry basket to impart the

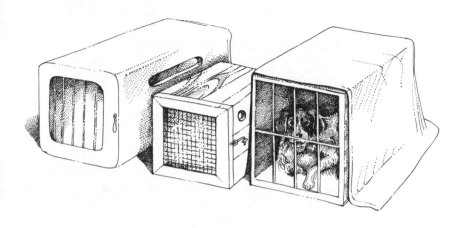

Figure 4–2 The most common kinds of dens are (from left to right) fiber glass carriers designed for travel; homemade crates constructed from sturdy lumber, screening, or hardware cloth; and manufactured metal wire or bar cages. Because the latter are open on all sides, cover the top and three sides with a blanket or cloth to make a more secure haven for your dog.

entire family's scent to it. Rubbing it with your hands before you give it to the dog also works well. This toy is your way of saying, "Don't worry, I'll be back."

Keep in mind that dogs have incredible internal clocks and if there's a boisterous homecoming followed by immediate feeding and a play session at five each evening, the dog's anticipation of it will begin to build in the late afternoon. If we get held up in traffic, stop to do some shopping, or have dinner with a friend, the dog (crated or not) will be an emotional time bomb. Uncrated dogs are more likely to be destructive during this brief interval than the rest of the day combined; and both crated and uncrated animals are apt to resort to nervous licking and chewing to dissipate the tension and frustration.

Setup Training: Poor Sportsmanship or Smart Thinking?

One of the best training techniques for weekend dog owners is the setup. As the name implies, this involves setting the dog up, deliberately creating conditions likely to result in negative behavior, then immediately dealing with the behavior within the thirty- to sixty-second retention span. Some weekend dog owners may think setting up a dog smacks of bad sportsmanship, but that's an owner, not a dog problem. Imagine Karen leaving her most tantalizing shoe right beside Rudy while she nonchalantly reads a magazine nearby. The dog sniffs the shoe, licks it, then takes the toe in his mouth and begins chewing. Like lightning, Karen bolts from her chair to discipline or distract the dog at that critical instant. After daily setups for several weeks, Rudy learns not to chew shoes and Karen smiles a lot more when asked about her relationship with her pet.

Distraction Training

Many people find a sharp whistle or some distracting noisemaker an effective substitute for physical punishment. A noise can momentarily distract a dog from its behavior long enough for the owner to give a simple command: "Go get your ball, Rudy!" Lavish praise is used to reinforce the latter behavior.

Distraction training has the advantage that it requires no physical force. Therefore, negative behavior that is corrected in this manner is not dependent on the size or strength of the individual using it. When it is coupled with a simple but sure command the dog will obey, it is a most effective means of correcting problem behavior.

Distraction training may strike you as odd if you think in terms of *punishment* being *necessary* to overcome negative behavior. Although such negative reinforcement can be effective, it can also create fear and guilt. The nice thing about distraction training is that it stops negative behavior by replacing it with good behavior without punishing the dog.

Reinforcement Training

Reinforcement training merely takes advantage of what the pup or dog is going to do anyway by attaching a command to it. For example, young pups tend to follow anything that moves. This is a natural reflex that serves to keep the growing pup close to the mother dog: she moves, they move. We can use this simple reflex to teach the pup to come and walk on a leash (see Chapter 5).

Reinforcement training works superbly with very young pups. It does not create a battle of wills, nor does it punish wrong moves. In many ways such an approach creates a game or even a ballet between owner and dog. The pup responds to you; you respond to it; it responds to your response; and so on, all in a matter of a few seconds. Not only can you have fun anticipating these sequences, you'll have a well-trained dog as your own reward.

Rewards: All You Need Is Love

Never under any circumstances use food as a reward when training your weekend dog. As we will discover in the chapter on weekend dog nutrition, creating an association between food and *anything* else is one of the most tragic errors a weekend dog owner can make and one of the most complex for both owner and dog to rectify. A well-known professional trainer who spends a lot of time working with problem dogs claims he can always spot dogs trained with food rewards. "They're always on edge, always looking for something. They direct their attention toward the food rather than successful behavior or owner praise."

Compare painting the living room or finishing a difficult report because it poses a challenge—something you *want* to do to please your spouse or boss, or yourself—versus something you feel *forced* to do in order to be allowed to eat. When we use food rewards in training, that's our way of telling our dogs we don't believe learning and doing a good job offer sufficient reward. Substituting a food stimulus for more natural means of eliciting love, then coupling that food with a belief that learning isn't fun, entangles the training process in an emotional web. It's no wonder many weekend dog owners give up and send the dog to a professional trainer.

CHAPTER 5

Teaching Weekend Pups the Basics

*I*solation and inconsistency make training a weekend pup a unique challenge. Let's look in on a typical pup in a typical weekend environment.

A four-month-old female golden retriever pup, Lael, lives with Sara Carter and her daughter in a housing development where almost every household has a pet. Lael stays indoors when the Carters are gone. From within the house, she hears all kinds of things going on in *her* yard and around *her* house, but can do nothing about them, so her natural instinct to seek out and explore novel stimuli is totally frustrated. Furthermore, she can't obey her strong instinct to protect and mark her territory. Combining two such instincts with no natural outlet causes some unnatural consequences. Because Lael is attached to the Carters and their property, she wants to protect them. But what can she do from inside? Nothing but bark and chew the rug. Sometimes she hears something so frightening, she even

wets and soils, the natural way for a pup to mark its territory (see Chapter 6).

At first, Sara attributes the chewing, barking, and wetting
to normal puppy behavior, but when it persists, she decides the pup is bored in her absence and resolves to tire
Lael out each morning. Shortly before leaving for work
and school, Sara and her daughter take Lael out for a long
walk and play vigorous, exciting catch-and-chase games
with her. Then they return her to the house.

"Now you be a good pup while we're gone. No messes,
do you hear? You take good care of the house and we'll
be right back!"

All of this stimulation plus the emotional farewell lead
Lael to think, *Wow, it's play time!* But suddenly everyone's
gone and there's no one to play with. All charged up with
nothing to do, Lael starts chewing on the rug the minute
Sara's car leaves the driveway. With their high-energy play
session, the Carters have unwittingly lit a short fuse on a
big behavioral bomb. Imagine giving a four-year-old boy a
similar play session and pep talk, then leaving him alone
in an empty house. It's the same kind of tension-producing
situation for a puppy.

After biting a foot-square chunk of carpet and reducing
it to a pile of threads, Lael curls up and takes a nap until
she hears Sara's car coming up the driveway. Lael bounds
to the door, but comes to a screeching halt when Sara begins screaming, "God, no! Not my mother's rug!"

The next day, pup and people repeat the performance,
only this time Lael proves she's not as dumb as her owners
think. The pup still grinds up another square foot of carpet, but because Lael associates her owners' anger with the
way she greeted them, she changes her greeting. Tucking
her tail tightly against her abdomen and squatting low, she
assumes the position of submission dogs use to say, *I want
to please you. I want to do whatever you want me to do.
Please don't hurt me.* One look at the cowering pup and
the Carters automatically assume Lael is acting guilty be-

cause she chewed the rug six hours earlier. The Carters and Lael may be talking to each other, but they certainly aren't communicating. And because they're not getting each other's message, the chances of any positive change are zero.

Within this scenario we see that Lael's isolation and lack of confidence are causing much of her negative behavior. We can also see how the Carters' failure to understand the pup's normal retention span is starting them off in a most discouraging relationship with their pup. Although pups as a group tend to be curious and willing to learn, all lack experience; and experience forms the foundation of confidence. Practically the only ways to instill confidence in a pup are denning or training, and weekend pup owners often have to do both. As mentioned in Chapter 4, denning takes the pressure off the animal while simultaneously protecting our furnishings from destructive behavior.

Denning Relieves Tension

When Sara finally decides to crate Lael while she and her daughter are gone, the first benefit they notice is the relief they feel knowing there will be no mess to clean up and no nightly screaming session with the pup. When Lael's in her crate, she's safe; she doesn't have to worry about all those crowded neighborhood noises. Although Sara and her daughter initially considered the crate a prison, Lael doesn't agree. Like many dogs who are denned, Lael prefers the crate when her owners are gone.

Build Confidence
to Eliminate Isolation Behavior

To build confidence in weekend pups, teach them to respond to simple commands. Dogs, like people, like to succeed. When Lael learns to come, sit, or lie down and sees how happy that makes the Carters, she feels happy too. When Lael learns to remain seated even when frightened

by events around her, she feels successful because of her
owners' lavish praise, and her confidence grows. The
more confidence Lael feels, the more it takes to upset her;
and as the number of things that upset Lael decreases, the
amount of stress on the pup decreases accordingly.

Let's take one method, reinforcement training, and use
it to teach Lael to come, sit, and lie down.

Teaching the Weekend Pup to Come

If the Carters put a collar and leash on Lael, establish
eye contact, and tug, like the majority of pups Lael will
probably dig in with her back feet, and may even whimper
or howl in fright. At that point, Sara must overcome her
guilt and embarrassment, if she's doing this in some public
place, and decide whether to drag the pup toward her in
this obviously unhappy state or skip the whole thing. If she
uses reinforcement training, Sara's approach is quite different. She hooks a lightweight, longer leash to Lael, calls her
quite cheerfully, *then turns her back on the pup* and begins running. At first she feels a little tug as the pup holds
back, but soon the following reflex takes over and Lael is
running at her side. Over a period of time, Sara can
shorten the leash and add quick turns to the pace to teach
the pup to remain at her side.

The running technique also works well for puppies who
are shy. There's a small shopping center in my area that's
a great place for weekend dog owners to socialize their
shy pets. While one family member gets the groceries, another runs the pup through the crowd, keeping up cheerful encouragement. To be sure, shy pups may require
more of a mad dash at first and may tend to rivet their
gaze on their owner's feet, but after a while the pace can
be slowed as the pup gains more confidence.

Using Mimicry to Teach a Pup to Sit

Another form of reinforcement training takes advantage
of the fact that many puppies mimic human behavior. We

move, they move; we sit down, they sit down. So when Sara gets up to get a snack during half-time, she keeps an eye on Lael. If Lael follows Sara with her gaze and starts to get up, Sara sneaks in a quick "Come, Lael" and then lavishly praises the pup when she does. When Sara sits down and sees the pup's rear end start to drop, a "Sit, Lael. Good dog!" is in order.

"Lie Down, Lael"

Teaching a pup to lie down can utilize both the pup's following reflex and the mimicking response. If you have a pup in a sitting position and quickly raise your hand from its nose to above its head and then drop it quickly to the floor, most pups will follow it, their front paws sliding forward. I find this technique works well on my stainless steel examining table. I suspect this is so because in addition to responding to the following reflex, the pups feel more secure lying down when they're elevated. An old table works just as well. What you want is a hard, smooth surface that promotes effortless forward sliding of those front feet—not some upholstered couch or chair that encourages the pup to dig in with its rear ones.

When taking advantage of mimicry, recognize that lying down is the natural sequel to sitting. Once Lael is seated beside Sara for the second half of the game, she'll invariably get tired and want to lie down. At the instant those front legs begin to slide into the down position, Sara should say, "Down, Lael. Good girl!"

When using reinforcement training, be careful to reinforce the desired behavior with proper commands *and* lavish praise—*consistently*. For example, try to apply the same words to the same act every time that act occurs. Don't say "Lie down" one time and "Down" the next. Pick the shortest possible command because you don't have much time to sneak your command in between the pup's initiating and completing an act. Above all, be lavish, sincere, and consistent with praise. Pups thrive on it and will learn much more quickly if they know you're pleased by their success.

Puppy Protégés

Don't be discouraged if all your reinforcement training seems to fall apart when your puppy reaches five or six months of age. First of all, the pup is losing the strong following reflex; second, it's gaining confidence. In many ways, pups at this age are similar to preteens, wanting to be independent but not quite sure of themselves. Like the preteen, the pup will often put its owner's patience to the test: *I've been around long enough to know that food and love are pretty sure things around here. I wonder if I have to do that come, sit, and stay stuff to keep it coming?*

The weekend pup owner must remain firm and consistent in his or her expectations of, and demands on, both trainer and pup. Don't give in. If the pup starts taking off when you call it to come, put a leash on it and start the training from the beginning again. If it refuses to sit or stay, keep working with it until it does. If you give up after ten minutes today, there's a good chance the pup will hold out for twenty minutes tomorrow. Once the pup understands that food and love do not depend on good behavior, but that you expect good behavior nonetheless, this phase will quickly pass.

Public vs. Private Education

Should you train your weekend pup or send it to obedience school? The answer depends on commitment, time, and money. If you do not enjoy daily repetitive work, then you'll quickly grow bored with training. Similarly, if your schedule includes hectic evening and weekend activities, you may be unable to supply the consistent training needed to ensure a well-behaved dog. Professional training costs money, but it can be a wise investment, paying off in long-lasting good behavior.

Many training books advise owners to establish control over their pups by teaching them simple commands such as come, sit, and stay. Although that works, some weekend dog owners face complicated problems later on because they were never able to teach the pup such commands in the first place. Of course, a problem dog takes more time to teach simple commands than the happy-go-lucky pup. In such cases, good professional training may be more than worth the cost, even if you have to scrimp and save to afford it.

Halfway between the do-it-yourself dog trainer with his or her how-to book and professional trainers fall group classes offered by many kennel clubs. These usually involve six to ten weekly sessions where owner and dog learn the basics together. For many weekend dog owners, such courses offer an ideal solution. The minimal time and money involved serve as incentives to stick with it and get the job done. As with setup training, it can be a fun social event for you and your dog. Most of what such courses teach appears in many dog training books currently on the market, but often we weekend dog owners find we're a little more consistent and conscientious if we know we have to face our friends each week to show them what we and our dogs have accomplished. In some areas you'll find excellent courses specifically for young pups. Remember, what you can teach a pup in a matter of weeks may take months or even years to accomplish with an adult dog.

Your veterinarian can offer other sources of training assistance. Because of the surge of behavioral problems that plague our weekend dog society, many vets have developed an interest in training. When you take your new pup in for routine vaccinations, discuss behavioral problems; these may affect your pup's total health as much as temperature and heart rate. Even if the vet cannot give specific advice, he or she should be able to refer you to those who can.

The Student Pup's Dilemma

No discussion of training techniques would be complete without mentioning the brilliant work done by William Campbell (*Behavior Problems in Dogs,* American Veterinary Publications, Inc., 1975). In his book, Campbell describes how even very young puppies consider both a hissing noise and pressure on the back very threatening sensations capable of eliciting a fear response. It is believed that these two sensations are those a wild pup associates with impending attack by snakes or the grasp of a predator. Presumably, then, these were originally canine protective mechanisms. We also recognize that a dog's hearing is much more sensitive than ours, enabling it to hear at seventy-five feet what we lose track of after seventeen feet.

Enter the traditional dog owner, John Doe, gung ho to teach his pup to sit. John stares at the pup hard, puts his face about a foot from its nose, and hisses, "Sit!" in a voice that undoubtedly sounds like a megaton cobra to the pup. The pup freezes. John repeats the command, this time even more loudly, *"I said, sit!"* and simultaneously forces the pup's rear to the ground. Instead of giving the pup any reason to sit, John has in fact given it three stimuli (hissing, loud noise, touch) that all tell it to freeze, fight, or run, the pup's primary responses to fear. The last thing the pup would instinctively want to do under such circumstances is sit quietly.

It is, as Campbell notes, a tribute to the stability of domestic dogs, and their bond to us, that any ever learned to sit! Not only do pups so trained have to learn the act itself, they have to overcome the aversion to the fearful stimuli the owner introduces, as well as figure out what the owner really wants them to do. Weekend dog owners have enough problems without creating new ones. Be aware of the pup's normal responses and take advantage of them. Above all, don't expect your dog to immediately understand what you're thinking, anymore than you immediately understand what *it's* thinking. Learn to communicate before you begin to train.

The most important thing about training a weekend pup is knowing what kind of behavior you want, what kind of life-style the dog will experience, and how much effort you're willing or able to invest. Once you know what you want and whether you or someone else can achieve that goal, you're well on your way.

CHAPTER 6

Housebreaking the
Weekend Dog

*E*very new weekend dog owner suffers through a phase
during which life seems to revolve around the dog's
stool and urine. The longed-for weekend rolls around but
instead of romping in the park with Thunderball, you're
moping around the house wondering why you can't stop
your dog's soiling the rug or the basement. Nor can you
cheer yourself up by inviting friends over after work because you know they'll be horrified by those yellow-
stained papers in the corner and the distinctive odor that
permeates your house. However, you don't have to live
like that unless you want to. Rather, you can let your dog's
natural cycle work for you instead of against you, making
housebreaking a lot simpler for you and your weekend
dog.

The Gastrocolic Reflex

Dogs themselves have three completely different views of their own stool and urine. What humans define as waste products from normal digestion, dogs experience as an involuntary nerve response to anything ingested, a primitive expression of love, and a sort of organic fence to mark territorial boundaries. Few dog owners realize the importance of the involuntary response called the gastrocolic reflex. The gastro (stomach) colic (posterior intestinal) reflex describes the ability of anything placed in the stomach to stimulate activity throughout the entire digestive system. Whenever a dog nibbles food or sips water, it sets in motion a routine sequence that inevitably results in urination and defecation. Doesn't it seem obvious that if we control the dog's food and water intake, we control its urine and stool production, too?

This especially applies to young puppies, whose circular muscles (sphincters) controlling the urinary bladder and rectum develop more slowly than other muscles. Because two- to three-month-old pups lack sufficient sphincter control, their housebreaking involves regulating *when* they urinate and defecate as well as where.

A Sign of Respect

When her pups finish a round of nursing, the mother dog gently flips each one over to clean it. As she laps the area around the anus, vagina, or penis, she stimulates the production of urine and feces which she immediately ingests to keep the nest area clean. Consider this from the pup's point of view: its first act of giving in response to another being involves urine and stool. Although a biological act, this primitive association greatly affects behavior. In older animals it manifests itself as spontaneous urination and/or defecation whenever the dog feels strong emotions, such as happiness to see its owner, or fear when encountering any sort of threat. Haven't we all seen dogs that wet every time they get excited? *This behavior always pleased Mom, and I want to please you, too!* If the owner doesn't understand the unique canine point of view, communication between dog and owner will quickly break down.

No Trespassing

Dogs also use urine and stool to mark territorial boundaries. Even young puppies feel compelled to establish and protect their territory. When a dog wets or soils in its own kitchen or backyard, it's just posting a "No Trespassing" sign for other dogs: *Go away. This is my home.* How can owners use these canine orientations to their advantage when housebreaking their pets? All it takes is a little patience and understanding.

Let's see how the gastrocolic reflex, and the maternal and territorial instinct responses affect one couple's attempts to housebreak their weekend dog. Jim and Linda Morrow get Yoda, an Airedale mix, when the puppy is eight weeks old. At first they give her the run of the house, but she creates so many puddles and piles overnight or in their absence that they decide to limit her freedom. Because deep-pile carpet covers every floor in their house except the kitchen, Linda and Jim naturally decide to keep the pup there at night and during the day when they are gone.

A pattern soon develops: Jim and Linda say goodnight to the pup, pet her fondly, fill her water bowl with fresh water, toss her a few biscuits, and go upstairs to bed. About two hours later, the Morrows' neighbors let their tomcat out to ravage the neighborhood. Yoda hears him but can't see him, frustrating her to the point where she squats and wets, then defecates to send the cat a message that he'd better not come into *her* house. Having posted her territory, Yoda munches a few biscuits and laps up some water. A short while later she responds to the gastrocolic reflex by depositing another pile and making another puddle.

When Yoda hears Linda coming downstairs the next morning, she rushes to greet her owner, but Linda ignores the tail-wagging pup and frowns at the puddles and piles. "Bad dog! Bad dog!" she yells, pushing the pup's nose into the nearest mess. She makes Yoda sit next to her while she cleans it up.

Again that night, the Morrows isolate Yoda in the kitchen with her biscuits and water, their neighbor puts out the obnoxious cat, and the pup repeats her performance. But not exactly. The next morning Yoda shows Jim and Linda that she's no dummy. She's learned something. When she hears Linda coming downstairs, Yoda thinks, *Gee, I was really happy to see Linda yesterday, but something about the way I greeted her really upset her. Today I'll greet her the way Mom taught me. That'll make her happy!*

As Linda enters the kitchen, Yoda assumes the position of total submission and respect—ears back, tail tucked tightly against her tummy, squatting and dribbling urine. Her mother would have been proud! Unfortunately, Linda looks from puppy to puddles to piles and shouts, "Bad, bad Yoda! See, Jim, the little bitch knows she did something wrong. She looks so guilty!"

Then Linda sticks the pup's nose in the nearest pile, scolding her loudly while she cleans up. The inevitable conflict between the dog's normal physiological and behavioral needs and the clean all-American home puts Yoda on the road to becoming one of the hundreds of thousands of unhousebroken dogs in this country.

What Went Wrong?

First of all, by making both food and water freely available to their puppy, the Morrows are guaranteeing a free-flowing supply of urine and stool. Don't fight the gastrocolic reflex; let it work for you. Put the pup (or dog) on a strict food and water schedule so you can reasonably predict when elimination will occur. And don't be lazy. For example, if Linda and Jim drag out of bed at six A.M. Monday through Friday to feed and walk Yoda, they should follow the same schedule on Saturday and Sunday. Nothing confuses a weekend dog more than two completely different patterns during housebreaking. Consistency not only aids training, it also helps keep natural biological responses on a predictable schedule. Maintaining strict feeding schedules during the week and on weekends may seem like a pain in the neck; but if you stick it out for a few weeks, your dog will be set for life.

A Message for Mom

The second error the Morrows make is misreading Yoda's submissive behavior. As we discussed in Chapter 4, dogs have short retention spans; Yoda will not connect Linda's yelling to her urinating and defecating hours before. Not only will Linda see no positive results from her anger, she damages the pup's confidence by seemingly scolding her for the behavior she displayed in the thirty to sixty seconds prior to Linda's angry outburst. No larger communication gap exists between owner and dog than that which occurs when the owner views a pup's submissive urination as a sign of defiance, spitefulness, or stupidity. The dog is really saying: *I want to please you.*

Another major communication breakdown takes place when the Morrows make Yoda watch them clean up the mess. Many people believe that when messes are made, the mess-maker must watch the cleanup. Owners following this logic think they're sending a clear message to the pup: *See all the trouble your messing causes me?* Will this make the dog feel guilty? Hardly. The pup views the cleanup process in terms of its nursing experience: *Boy, look at her collecting all my presents, just like Mom. I must be doing good. I wish she'd stop yelling, though. Why does she always stick my nose in it before she accepts it? That must be something humans do when they share stool-gifts.*

To avoid such mixed communication, get the pup out of the area before you begin cleaning up. Does it make you feel better having the pup there? That's normal, but bear in mind that you will invariably fail to lay a guilt trip on your dog about any urinating and defecating that occurred hours before. Even if you could, would guilt solve the problem?

The Territorial Backfire

Finally, by isolating Yoda in the kitchen, Linda and Jim create an unnecessarily high-tension environment for her, one in which she is in conflict with two of her strongest needs, the need to be with others and the need to establish and protect her territory. Despite Yoda's perceptual ability (sight, hearing, and smell) her youthful lack of experience can cause her to misapply territorial marking. It's the equivalent of telling your best friend: "Look, I want you to house-sit for me next week. I live in a twenty-three-room glass house on five hundred acres at the end of a dirt road. I don't believe in locks, I don't believe in weapons, but I do have an eight-million-dollar art and jewelry collection. Oh, did I mention that I ratted on the mob in New Jersey and they know where I live?"

To make matters worse, the more attached Yoda grows to her home, the more likely she will be tempted to mark it when isolated or stressed. Marking behavior does not always indicate fear; it can express aggressiveness: *Beware, this is mine and I'll fight for it!* In puppies, however, marking behavior usually expresses a lack of confidence. As the pup matures with experience, the number of perceived threats decreases and confidence increases. As this happens, the shy, reluctant pup will begin to extend its territory beyond the house and into the yard. It's all right for

Yoda to mark the four corners of the yard, but not the four corners of the kitchen. Still, marking behavior never expresses hate and spite toward humans. Those are people, not dog, feelings.

The easiest way for Jim and Linda to begin housebreaking Yoda properly is to let the pup sleep with them. Many dogs that have wet and soiled in the kitchen or basement for weeks will become instantly housebroken with this approach because most young puppies and many dogs view people as dominant. When Yoda sleeps beside Linda and Jim, she doesn't give a hoot about the neighbor's cat. If it doesn't bother Jim and Linda, it doesn't bother Yoda.

If the thought of sleeping with your dog in the room repulses you, you will not be happy with this approach. On the other hand, if you don't mind having your dog actually sleep in your bed, you may find housebreaking even more simple. In addition to removing isolation stress, allowing the pup to sleep with you takes advantage of another very strong canine instinct that insists: *You don't mess where you eat or sleep.* Because most dogs attach the same specialness to their owner's sleeping quarters as they do to their own, they will seldom mess on the bed, or even in the bedroom.

Is there a catch? Unfortunately, yes. Each dog seems to develop its own idea about how much area exceeds its protective ability, even in the owner's presence. While some pups feel comfortable in the average eleven-by-fifteen-foot bedroom, others demand a smaller area just big enough for them, a blanket, and a favorite toy. You can accommodate the latter pup by attaching it with a short leash to the leg of the bed. Such short-leashing allows you to easily reach down and reassure the puppy during the night if necessary. However, do not use this technique when the pup is alone; active pups can easily become entangled in even the shortest leashes. But don't hesitate to do it during the night when you're there. If the pup messes, the leash is too long; shorten it. Remember, you're simply trying to convert a threatening area that *must* be marked into a sacred sleeping area that must *not.*

Denning Makes Good Use of Natural Instincts

If short-leashing bothers you or doesn't get results, crating or denning will almost always work. Only human prejudice keeps denning from being the most popular means of house-training the weekend dog. Although many people associate crates or kennels with jails and punishment, crating actually recognizes that most pups and many adult dogs yearn for a safe haven, a den where they needn't worry about protecting territory. Unfortunately, we weekend dog owners are such suckers for guilt that the thought of imprisoning our dogs often feeds our beliefs that we're being cruel and inhumane, that we've no business owning a dog in our weekend society.

Denning is not cruel and inhumane. Not only does it offer an effective way to housebreak a pup, it does so within three to four weeks. On the other hand, the pup confined in the larger, supposedly more humane kitchen may never become housebroken. The weekend dog owner faces these choices:

- Crate or kennel the dog for three to four weeks with a good chance of housebreaking it for life.
- Keep the dog in the kitchen and prepare yourself to have it continue urinating and defecating in the house.
- Stick the dog outdoors twenty-four hours a day and pray it doesn't run away or pick up other bad habits such as barking, digging, and chewing.

My clients and patients have proven that denning is neither cruel nor inhumane. Those who den their pups from the beginning usually find that long after the pups are trustworthy in the house, they voluntarily go into the crates for peace and quiet or when they see the owners preparing to go out. Would this happen if the animals consider the crate offensive? Many adult dogs continue to use their crates daily although the owners have not needed to close the crate door for years. I know one owner who dismantled the crate and put it in the garage after her dog was well behaved; she found her dog lying mournfully beside it the next day. What some people view as a form of punishment, most pups view as a haven.

If you crate a pup but remain in its presence, it will probably make a fuss. Remember, dogs are social animals that want to be with other animals or people. On the other hand, once you're gone or sleeping, most pups prefer a secure sleeping place of their own rather than a big scary kitchen or basement filled with unfamiliar sights, sounds, and smells.

One last word about crating: if the pup messes in the crate, it's too big. For some pups, a very thin line separates how much room is big enough to offer comfort but not too big to require marking. Some pups need a tiny space to feel secure; others need a larger one. For example, I have a friend who lives a mere block from the police station in a seventeenth-floor, two-room apartment with four locks on the door. Her toy poodle sleeps in a crate the size of a large shoe box. Anything bigger it soaks with urine. Another friend, Art Fitzwilliam, doesn't feel safe except on his ten acres of land on a dead-end road where he doesn't have to lock his doors. His dog, Duke, would die rather than mess Art's twenty-by-twenty-three-foot bedroom, but will mark every doorway with urine if given the run of the house. If your dog soils its expensive fiber glass carrier, don't throw it, the pup, and this book out. Just keep filling the kennel with cardboard boxes to take up the excess space until the pup feels secure.

To sum up, these are the common natural behavior responses affecting housebreaking and their causes:

Response	*Cause*
Gastrocolic response	Elimination of waste following eating and/or drinking
Submissive urination and/or defecation	Sign that dog acknowledges another dog or person as dominant
Territorial marking	Use of urine and stool to signal other animals regarding ownership of property

Special Housebreaking Problems

Paper-Training

Before leaving house-training, let's explore a few special problems, beginning with paper-training. In most cases, paper-training simply means you train the pup twice—once to go on newspaper and again to go outdoors. We weekend dog owners have so little spare time, we shouldn't waste it housebreaking our dogs twice. Besides, paper-training introduces complications. A pup can tell the difference between inside and outside more easily than between newspaper and vinyl floor covering. I even know owners who use paper-training because *they* don't like to go outdoors. No one likes to be out in a drenching downpour or snowstorm waiting for the dog to find a proper spot to relieve itself. On the other hand, these horrible weather conditions often encourage pups to perform more rapidly so they can get back inside their warm, dry homes.

Worst of all, paper-training confuses dogs. When we train a dog, we provide the simulus (the clean newspaper) so the dog will make the proper response (urinate and/or defecate on the paper) and receive a reward (lavish praise or petting). If such training succeeds, the dog will continue using the paper to please its owner despite the fact that it has developed the necessary muscle control to hold its waste for long periods.

I recently received a frantic phone call from a client demanding that I immediately castrate her four-month-old beagle, George, because he was lifting his leg on the furniture. Leg lifting to squirt small amounts of urine on objects is normal marking behavior for sexually mature male dogs, but at four months, George certainly didn't fall into this category. After questioning the distraught owner, I learned that a predictable consequence of paper-training had occurred. The previous evening the owner's husband had retired after dinner to his favorite chair in the living room to read the paper and watch television. News being news and television being television, he soon dozed off, his paper slipping to the floor—almost. Usually George remains in the kitchen to help his owner tidy up, but last night he sauntered into the living room looking for some fun. *Ah ha! What's this nice clean paper resting up against the chair? I know what that's for!*—squirt! Had George wet on the flat paper on the kitchen floor, his owner would have hugged and kissed him as jubilantly as ever, but because George wet against the side of a chair, she wants him castrated. The moral? As far as pups are concerned, paper is paper. Help your pup avoid having to make such subtle distinctions by training it to go outdoors.

The Dog That Should Be Trained but Isn't

Many times busy people get adult dogs from humane societies with the idea that these animals will be housebroken. Actually, quite often the opposite is true. Many animals wind up in such places because they *aren't* housebroken. Unfortunately, the original owners' feelings of guilt and inadequacy prevented them from revealing the problem to the personnel of the animal shelter. If the shelter places such a dog in a small kennel (den), no problem will be detected until the new owners find the puddles and piles in their homes.

At this point the situation becomes complicated. People who take adult dogs from shelters or from friends often believe they are saving the animal from an untimely death, which may be true. However, what happens when the object of our benevolent act ruins our house, causing us great anguish? Do we send it back to certain death? Do we submit to the sort of strenuous training regimen we wanted to avoid in the first place, knowing it will take much longer to get results with an older dog? Any would-be owner of an unhousebroken secondhand dog must confront these issues before taking responsibility for the animal. If our feelings about what will happen to the dog outweigh our aversion to house-training and temporary messes, then training can begin. If not, don't accept the animal, for your relationship with it will surely turn sour.

If you decide to keep the dog, begin by putting it on a strict food and water schedule, regulating its opportunities to relieve itself. Always tailor the dog's schedule to yours; if you can't be home *every* day to feed and walk the dog at noon during the week, then don't do it on weekends. Such inconsistencies will only complicate the housebreaking process. Recognize that physiological control in adult dogs poses less of a problem than territorial marking. Limit the territory. When you're home with the dog, leash it at all times. If you must leave it alone for even an instant, short-leash it to a table leg. If you're going out, crate it.

Owners of unhousebroken dogs saved from the pound invariably compare denning to the life the dog led there. But that's often because they don't have the confidence to recognize that their own love and presence elevate the quality of the dog's life tremendously. Whenever you return, even if it's only from a trip to another room, praise the dog and pet it. Although it will not associate your praise with not messing, this will help to establish the strong bond that inevitably aids any sort of training. Confidence in the strength of that bond will sustain both owner and dog through the months it may take to housebreak an adult dog.

In the next chapter we will talk about denning to prevent all sorts of negative behavior. Because adult dogs that are not housebroken often display other behavior problems, denning enables the weekend dog owner to resolve more than one at a time.

Dogs That Have Fallen Off the Wagon

Almost invariably, housebroken dogs that revert to soiling do so in response to some change in the household. Most commonly this involves the addition of a new person or animal, or the dog's suddenly being left alone. Although house soiling in response to environmental change may strike owners as spiteful, it usually indicates quite the opposite. Consider the case of shy little cairn terrier Scruffy Coleson, whose owners had their first child, a son, after eight years of nonparenthood. The day the new baby comes home, Scruffy begins soiling when left alone in the house. A lot of people might insist that Scruffy is justifiably jealous because she has been supplanted by a competitor. Doesn't that sound like a Dependent view? I prefer to gauge Scruffy's motives from the Bonded point of view.

The more attached the dog grows to its owners, the more thoroughly it will protect its owner's property.

Let's speculate how Scruffy might view the new baby's arrival. First of all, the infant spends most of his time lying on his back soiling his diapers. *This "pup" wants me to take care of it,* thinks Scruffy, seeing the infant's behavior in terms of submissive behavior in dogs. Scruffy also watches the Colesons' interaction with their son and recognizes he's quite important to them. *Boy, I want to be sure nothing happens to him!* decides the dog. Finally, Scruffy has spent most of her life in a household where she was alone five days a week while her owners worked. Since the birth of the baby, June Coleson only works part-time. She also belongs to a baby-sitting co-op, so some afternoons there are as many as five young children in the Coleson home.

After having a predictable and fairly quiet life for so long, Scruffy finds these comings and goings very confusing and can't quite handle the increased protective burden. Because this frightens her, she solves her problem by shrinking her territory. In short, she's saying that she wants to take care of the Coleson household, but the thought of protecting the yard, the house, *and* the baby overwhelms her. Denning gently takes the protective role out of the dog's control and allows her to relax.

To be sure, some dogs' motives may not be so pure; they do respond like jealous children. However, those are rare exceptions. The only dog I ever encountered that acted antagonistic toward a new arrival was one that had exhibited other behavior problems in the past.

House soiling may also occur when an individual the dog perceives as dominant or threatening moves into the household. Irene Morris, a systems analyst, lives alone with her two-year-old Boxer, Boris. Irene's son, Joe, enlisted in the armed forces shortly before she got the dog and Boris has never seen him. When Joe comes home, the dog takes one look at the uniform and wets all over the floor. That night, while Joe and his mother are visiting friends, the dog wets in Irene's bedroom.

Again, this is not a spiteful dog showing its dislike for Joe and Irene, but one that has lived with a low-keyed, nondominant working owner and is just encountering his first dominant human. Because he lacks confidence, Boris immediately squats and wets to show Joe he recognizes the man's superiority. However, the dog also feels a need to protect Irene and her house, which has been his sole responsibility during the hours she works or is away from home. So, he marks her room. It's his way of saying, *I cede everything to that dominant human; however, I will protect Irene.* Whether Boris acts out of love or merely views Irene as his property matters little. The fact is, he's not trying to punish her.

In order to solve this problem, Joe must become less dominant in the dog's eyes. For the first week, Joe totally ignores the dog, especially avoiding eye contact or speaking loudly, two acts that often elicit submissive urination. Simultaneously, Irene spends ten minutes twice daily putting Boris through his paces. Although she took him to obedience classes as a pup, Irene never felt any need to reinforce the training because Boris behaved so well in her calm household. What little negative or dominant behavior the dog displayed when she was home, Irene simply ignored. Because Boris never *had* to do anything for Irene, he soon forgot that she was in charge of the household. This caused no problem as long as Irene considered his behavior acceptable, but when he begins urinating in her bedroom, she has to let him know who's in charge.

The second week, Irene continues the daily training sessions with Joe silently sitting in the same room as Boris, ignoring the dog as usual. Joe sits on the floor to diminish his imposing six-foot height; whenever Boris comes close or shows any interest, Joe speaks softly and cheerfully to the dog, occasionally sneaking a quick glance. The process continues for as long as it takes Boris to come to Joe and start normal bonding.

The key words are patience and consistency; do it slowly, do it daily, and the dog will eventually come around. If Boris stops the submissive urination, but persists in marking the bedroom, shutting the bedroom door will often stop the behavior. If this is impossible, placing the dog's food and water dishes on the spot will often deter it. If none of these work or if the dog begins soiling elsewhere, it indicates that the dog's confidence has fallen so low only denning will relieve the tension and stop the behavior.

House soiling that begins when you start leaving your dog alone invariably reflects isolation behavior and territorial marking. If your dog uses one spot, you may block off that area or place the dog's feeding dishes on it. Again, denning will relieve the dog of the burden of suddenly increased isolation and protective responsibility.

Medical vs. Behavioral Problems

Weekend dog owners should be able to differentiate between three basic urination patterns: incontinence, infection, and marking. Incontinence is the inability to hold and release urine voluntarily. A dog suffering from this medical ailment will drop urine wherever it walks, and soak its own bedding wherever it sleeps. Urinary incontinence commonly affects older spayed females and may result from a lack of the female sex hormone estrogen. Estrogen replacement therapy usually resolves the problem. For males, or for females that do not respond to estrogen therapy, a complete diagnostic work-up may be necessary to determine the cause.

If the dog urinates frequent, small amounts it may have a bladder infection (cystitis). Cystitis differs from incontinence because the former involves voluntary urination. Animals with cystitis want to go out frequently to relieve themselves and may even break their house-training if they get so uncomfortable they can't wait for their owners to get home from work to let them out. However, they will not soil their beds.

If the dog always wets in the same one or two spots, it is most likely marking. Although urinary tract problems commonly crop up in older dogs, much geriatric in-house urination comes from territorial instincts. I have seen perfectly house-trained older dogs suddenly begin wetting on the mat by the kitchen door when the eldest child goes off to college or a new dog moves into the neighborhood. I can almost hear that stately fourteen-year-old springer spaniel saying, *I'll be damned if I'll fight for that backyard, but if something threatens my food and people, look out!* When you consider a fourteen-year-old dog's chances against an intruder, that's a pretty strong, though never spiteful, statement. For most elderly dogs, denning offers the most effective solution, but owners often can't bear to crate an animal that has behaved well for many years. They prefer to tolerate the behavior, because marking is usually within a limited area. Washable mats or flooring may be placed in such areas for easy cleaning.

Limiting the Area

Let's suppose you've trained your weekend dog to go outdoors most of the time. While you're out there with it, keep it on a leash and train it to use one small corner of the yard, even if you have five hundred acres (*especially* if you have five hundred acres). This saves you from doing little jumping dances when you mow the lawn and keeps the yard enjoyable for children and friends. You'll reap other rewards, too: the larger the area in which your dog urinates and defecates, the bigger the territory it must protect. Also, don't take your pup to the park at the end of the block to relieve itself, then expect it to remain calm when it sees your neighbor's dog hightailing it for that same park. Conflicting canine calling cards in the same area can cause a lot of tension and frustration. Not only might dominant dogs fight in such an area, submissive ones might grow apprehensive about relieving themselves there at all. One of my patients refuses to urinate or defecate in its yard in the city because numerous neighborhood dogs use it, too. Although beautifully paper-trained, the dog will not go anywhere outdoors in the city. However, she never messes indoors at the family's secluded summer house in rural Maine. For some dogs, competition can be downright intimidating. For others, it's a reason to wet and soil more. Watch male dogs in a common area sometime; you'll be amazed how many times a dog can go.

Good medical reasons also dictate limiting the elimination area to a small portion of your own yard. Intestinal parasites are not uncommon in dogs, and it's useless to worm a dog if it returns to the same area cluttered with infective stool. We weekend owners have better things to do with our free time than comb a half-acre lot looking for dog waste, or worming all the dogs in the neighborhood to protect our own. Limit the area, limit the problems, and simplify your life.

Before we go on to the next chapter, here are some housebreaking points to remember:

- Give food and water on a strict schedule seven days a week.
- If the pup is not with you, confine it.
- Don't let the pup see you clean up the mess.
- Take the pup to the same area in your yard to relieve itself.
- If you walk your dog, have it urinate and defecate in your yard *first*. Don't let it stop during the walk.

CHAPTER 7

Breaking Bad Habits and Teaching Old Dogs New Tricks

*T*he concept of *mutual* good should always guide dog training, but especially when it involves altering existing behavior in an adult dog. The first thing to understand is that our beliefs affect the way we approach a training problem. If we begin with the Independent belief that the dog behaves according to wild, alien instincts and *wants* to be out chasing cars rather than home with us, we'll automatically initiate a battle of wills that will invariably affect how we communicate with the dog.

If we view dogs as furry humanoids, we'll also have trouble successfully changing negative behavior because our own feelings may get in the way. But if we believe that dogs and people sometimes think alike and sometimes don't, training becomes much easier. Because both species thrive on praise and respect, learning can be quite enjoyable. If it's not fun for us, if we're not willing to learn, if we have no confidence in our pets' ability to learn and our ability to teach, no training program will succeed.

Analyzing the Problem

Study any behavioral problem before attempting to resolve it. A simple checklist can guide your evaluation:

- How do you feel about this problem?
- Do you have the time and patience to train an older dog?
- Is the problem related to isolation?
- Is the problem related to inconsistent training in the past?
- When did the problem start?

Inconsistency often results from our *feelings* about a problem. If you feel responsible for it ("Trinket chews the furniture because I leave her alone"), then you define the problem as unsolvable. Whether you accept total responsibility for your dog's behavior or none at all (Dependent versus Independent views), you'll have trouble breaking bad habits.

Owners holding strong Independent or Dependent beliefs about their dogs will find it easier to change *their* beliefs before they attempt to change their dogs. This may be accomplished in one of two ways: reworking your philosophy into a more flexible, Bonded one (see Chapter 3), or changing your attitude toward the problem. Let's consider the latter possibility. One can eliminate any problem by simply not classifying it as a problem. For example, Marty Shuman can say, "Curry's chewing is not the problem—the fact that it bothers *me* is the problem." If it doesn't bother Marty, it ceases to be a problem. Or take Adele Metzger: "The problem is not that Trinket chews or wets when I go out; the problem is that her behavior bothers *me*." If Marty and Adele decide to ignore the behavior, they've solved their problems. However, if a given behavior continues to be a source of embarrassment, anger, or guilt, the only solution lies in a complete reevaluation of one's philosophy.

Retraining an Older Dog

Despite the old saw, you *can* teach old dogs new tricks; all it takes is time and patience. What you can teach a young pup in weeks may take months or even years to teach an adult dog, particularly if you have to extinguish some negative behavior first. Often, untrained dogs in the two-to-four age group pose major problems because maturity cements certain habits and behaviors. If no one has established human bonding prior to this time, mature animals with sufficient vigor and confidence often don't want or need human interference. Although such a situation may persist for a dog's entire life, normal aging often slows it down and it grows more receptive to human companionship and training.

To train an older dog you must make it mutually rewarding. A dog that happily ran loose for five years, roaming miles each day and eating garbage, requires gentle and gradual convincing to stay home and eat kibble. Sure, you can clamp a chain on the dog and provide dry food on a take-it-or-leave-it basis, but that doesn't offer the animal any incentive to hang around if it slips its collar or breaks that chain. Though time-consuming, gradual feeding changes over several weeks or months is more likely to result in taming the stray garbage eater (see Chapter 9). Sometimes we want to improve a wrong diet or trait so badly, our enthusiasm overwhelms the dog. Whether or not we think garbage an inappropriate diet, many dogs consider it much more palatable than even the best quality commercial dog food. In order to adapt a garbage eater to a better diet, you may actually have to mix commercial dog food with garbage, gradually increasing portions of the desired food until you slowly wean the animal.

Changing an older dog's behavior often requires a series of intermediate steps, each one moving a little closer to the desired behavior. This takes time, *but you can combine your attack on one problem with an assault on another.* While gradually giving the garbage eater more good food and less junk, the owner can simultaneously teach the dog to respond to a command to come to the kitchen. Once the dog obeys the command indoors, the owner can move the training sessions outdoors. Always praise success. In an environment where both dog and owner succeed, a strong bond begins to form. If the dog learns over a period of time that coming when called stimulates joy, its owner has made much progress toward establishing a lasting trait. On the other hand, how much can owner or pet learn when the animal dangles from the end of a chain? Patience, praise, and love simplify and improve all aspects of weekend ownership, but especially when it comes to teaching old dogs new tricks.

When Did the Problem Start?

Knowing when the problem began gives us many clues about its cause and how to solve it. For example, if Trinket was always well behaved until Adele started leaving her alone on Thursdays, we know that the problem is related to Trinket's being alone. If Trinket is alone other days and is well behaved, then we can say the problem is related to her being alone on Thursdays. We can then begin to figure out what makes Thursday different from the other days of the week. "Why, that's the day the garbage man comes!" exclaims Adele.

In the last chapter we saw how Scruffy Coleson and Boris Morris began house soiling when a new infant and a dominant adult entered the household. Other dogs may begin chewing, barking, and other negative or even aggressive behavior under similar circumstances. New dogs in the neighborhood, unfamiliar sounds such as construction crews working in or around the house, severe storms which damage the house when the dog is home alone, are some of the many events that may precipitate negative behavior in a previously well-behaved dog.

Once you pinpoint when the negative behavior began and understand the reason why it occurred, you can re-create the favorable conditions preceding it or create new conditions to help accustom your dog to its new life-style. Sometimes denning the animal during this interval also helps relieve the tension.

Is the Problem Related to Isolation?

If the problem stems from isolation, you can either remove the isolation (provide acceptable company for the dog or allow it unlimited freedom) or use training or denning to remove the source of frustration. All problem behavior, but especially that caused by isolation, demands training, not only to undo the negative behavior but also to instill confidence in the dog. If a dog chews the furniture when left alone, you might stop the chewing by setting the dog up and consistently disciplining it when it chews, but you won't decrease the frustration and lack of confidence that led to the chewing in the first place. Sometimes teaching such a dog to come, sit, and stay will go a long way toward building confidence and thwarting the negative behavior. Remember, the more confidence a dog has, the more it takes to upset it and the more comfortable it feels when left alone.

Once Adele recognizes that Trinket's behavior results from the dog's isolation and lack of confidence, she decides to enroll her in obedience classes and get another dog. She chooses a male shepherd-mix puppy which she has neutered at six months. In a short time, the larger, more dominant dog gladly assumes a protective role when Adele is gone, leaving Trinket to sleep contentedly in her bed.

Although the companionship of another dog may reduce isolation behavior, owners should add another dog
cautiously, paying close attention to the relationship the
new dog will have with the existing pet as well as other
members of the family (see Chapter 11). When Marty Shuman's boss offers him a spayed female Samoyed the same
age as Curry, he unhesitatingly accepts, thinking the two
dogs will keep each other so busy neither will have time
to misbehave. However, the two dogs are so similar in
size, age, and experience that they bicker constantly for
the right to protect the territory. Bob Smith and Darlene
Colchik have two male Dobermans, one a year old, the
other three. The three-year-old totally runs the house although the younger one also exhibits protective instincts
when the older dog is gone; but when the two dogs are
together, the younger one does nothing but lap nervously
on his front paws and suck the comforter on the couch.
Two intelligent dogs coexisting in one household eventually develop a pack order; one becomes dominant with full
protective duties, leaving the submissive one with nothing
to do. Consequently, the dominant animal may appear very
well behaved and confident while the other looks like a
bundle of raw nerves. Although the less dominant dog may
supply companionship for the more dominant one, it
hardly makes life easier for the owner.

Was There Inconsistent Training in the Past?

Remember our bounding springer spaniel pup, Willow?
Willow belongs to fashion consultant Sue Jacobs, who
wears expensive clothing so she can't tolerate the jumping
behavior. Unfortunately, Sue only scolds Willow for jumping on workdays because on the weekend, Sue wears old
jeans and doesn't care if Willow comes flying into her
arms.

If the problem has arisen as a result of inconsistent
training, resolving it means you will have to change before

you try to change your dog. Sue finds it much easier to train Willow not to jump up after she realizes she contributes to the negative behavior by inconsistent disciplining. A dog's consistent response depends on the owner's consistency. All the setups and rolled newspaper swats in the world aren't going to keep Willow down if Sue coaxes her to jump up when she's wearing jeans. In fact, research indicates such inconsistency will actually keep negative behavior going *longer* than if Sue does nothing about it at all.

Owner inconsistency invariably leads to owner guilt, which, as we have seen, throws a big obstacle into weekend dog training. If we feel guilty because our work clothes or our furnishings mean a lot to us, we'll not calmly and consistently deal with an assault on them. If we feel guilty about leaving our dogs home alone all day, we'll not consistently respond to any negative behavior that occurs in our absence. If we feel guilty about owning a dog in a weekend environment, we'll spend more time creating excuses than solutions.

Making Learning Fun for
the Older Dog

Although learning should always be fun, it's especially important to keep this in mind when correcting problem behavior. Regardless of the problem behavior you wish to alter, always create a situation where both you and your dog can enjoy learning. Everyone enjoys success, so set things up in a way that allows success. If you don't have the time and patience for basics, send the dog to a professional for a good behavioral foundation you can reinforce at home. If the problem overwhelms you, select one small part to tackle first. Above all, make it fun. Make it a game that can include friends and relatives.

When Marty Shuman realizes the only way he's going to

stop Curry's isolation behavior is to set her up and distract her, he's worried. "I'll feel like a complete idiot," he groans to a co-worker. "Let's store some beer and cards in the shed behind your place," responds the friend. "Every so often we'll sneak up to the house, set up Curry, then go back to the shed for a few hands of poker." But Marty can't bring himself to do it.

Whether or not you approve of this method, it has more chance of succeeding than the hit-or-miss Independent approach Marty's inconsistently used in the past. Don't be embarrassed about including your friends and relatives in your retraining endeavors. Not only can they provide support, they can also help you retain the sense of humor, confidence, and consistency necessary to train your weekend dog.

Knowing When to Quit

An old German proverb says, "All beginnings are difficult," but sometimes stopping is even harder. Obviously, if we achieve our goal of a well-trained dog, we can relax and periodically reinforce the good behavior. However, what do you do when your life-style or the relationship with your dog conspires to thwart training? Then we face the same familiar choices:

- We can accept the behavior (including our feelings about it).
- We can change the way we feel about the behavior.
- We can have someone else train the dog.
- We can get rid of the dog.

If it's the right thing for you and your dog, quitting should not embarrass you. But how do you know when to quit? If chewing, digging, chasing cars, or jumping up bothers you, you must either change or change the behavior.

Although Marty Shuman acknowledges he simply doesn't

want to spend the necessary time to train Curry, he can't
accept things the way they are either. His furnishings and
the appearance of his house mean a great deal to him. It
bothers him very much that a dog exerts such a negative
influence on his feelings about himself and his home.
Once he accepts that he can't train Curry or change the
way he feels about the destruction of his property, he realizes he must decide whether to seek professional help.
He arranges an appointment with a professional trainer.
Marty tells the trainer how much time he's willing to
spend with the dog and asks about the nature of the re-
medial training and the necessary follow-through. He also
describes the extent of Curry's problem and how he handled it in the past. After hearing the trainer's recommendations, Marty lists the pros and cons of his relationship
with Curry:

Pros	Cons
Friendly	Destructive
Likes kids	Doesn't listen
Likes to play	Expensive
	Can't entertain friends at home
	Makes me angry
	Hates other dogs
	Chases cars

Marty soon realizes that the cons outnumber the pros.
With a feeling of deep regret, he decides to get rid of his
dog.

Getting rid of a dog is another one of those topics no
one wants to talk about. If you don't have friends or relatives in the country willing to take a problem dog, but
have been through hell with your pet, you'll undoubtedly
feel guilty about taking the dog to a humane society where
some other unsuspecting person may adopt it and experi-

ence the same headaches and heartaches as you. That leaves euthanasia.

It's a horrible dilemma. "If I hadn't taken Curry as a pup, someone else could have given her a good home and the attention she needed," sighs Marty. Maybe, maybe not. The fact remains that the quality of Marty's and Curry's life has deteriorated badly. What does Marty gain by keeping a dog that makes him miserable, a dog that he, in turn, makes more miserable? Nothing but misery. Hard as it may be, he must make his choice on the basis of what he believes to be right for him and Curry, not on what others think or tell him to do. Euthanasia is never an easy choice, but there are times when it may be the right one.

Setups for Success

Now that we know how to analyze problem behavior and our feelings about it, let's look at some common bad habits and see how we can use setups, distractions, and reinforcement training to resolve them. Let's begin with a typical weekend dog problem that many owners unwittingly create themselves.

The Chaser and Nipper

We all know people who encourage young pups to play tug-of-war, yet this popular game can result in problems down the line. Jim Morrow has played tug-of-war with Yoda since she was a pup. "Great exercise," he insists. But one morning, Linda oversleeps and runs down the hall to the shower, her nightgown flapping. Faithful Yoda, thinking it's all right to clamp onto something and shake it, and heeding a pup's instinct to chase anything that moves, decides Linda wants to play. "Yeow!" howls Linda, "that damned dog just bit me." Yoda may or may not have meant to clamp onto Linda's leg instead of her nightgown; to the pup it looked like a variation of a favorite game. I have seen tug-of-war-trained large breeds drag children from moving sleds and bicycles. When this happens, society labels the animal vicious whereas the dog obviously considers itself playful.

Jim and Linda can train Yoda not to chase and bite them by setting her up evenings and weekends when they needn't rush off to work. For the setup, Linda wears heavy socks and jeans underneath her gown. Whenever dealing with any problem behavior that includes possible biting or nipping, always wear heavy clothes, boots, gloves—whatever it takes to make you feel confident and secure. If you feel the least apprehensive about being hurt, you'll communicate those feelings to the dog. Don't worry if you look like an Arctic explorer during a heat wave in downtown Chicago; this little temporary inconvenience can earn you a well-trained dog.

Try to create setups that distract the dog from the negative behavior and substitute an acceptable one to hasten training. As Linda dashes down the hall, Jim stands nearby with Yoda's favorite toy, ready to distract the dog. Because Linda knows her motion attracts Yoda, she freezes the instant the dog rushes at her. With the moving stimulus suddenly gone, Yoda pauses, disoriented. At that instant, Jim enthusiastically calls the dog, waving the toy. When Yoda responds to his call, Jim pets her and gives her the toy. The Morrows repeat this performance until Yoda *expects* to be distracted whenever she sees Linda (or anyone) running and automatically goes to get her toy.

Softening a Hard-mouthed Dog

Because even unintentional biting can be so disastrous, I *strongly* discourage any kind of play that reinforces a dog's mouthiness. Playing tug-of-war or fetch, during which the owner tries to pull something from a dog's mouth, says to dogs, *Hang on hard!* To dogs, whose vision follows motion more than detail, an old towel used for tug-of-war play and a three-year-old's flapping coattail look pretty much alike. If your dog enjoys such games, stop playing them. Toss the ball or toy, but teach your dog to drop it before you throw it again. If the dog won't drop it, turn your back and walk away. After a while most dogs get bored and drop the toy. Then you can pick it up, praise the dog, and continue the game.

Although this seems like an excessively strong condemnation of one of the American dog owner's favorite pastimes, many shepherd breeders and trainers use a slogan that has value for us all: "Never teach a shepherd the power of its mouth." That's true for all breeds. Reinforcing hard-mouthed behavior is one of the most dangerous things a weekend dog owner can do. A dog that has been trained to clamp on, whether in play or attack work, requires *constant* supervision, the kind few weekend dog owners have the time to give. Owners of such unsupervised dogs must live with the realization that their pet could inadvertently or intentionally hurt someone at any time.

If you have a mouthy dog that likes to chew or lap hands, hang on to its lower jaw while maintaining eye contact with it, thanking it profusely for its wonderful gift. No hint of anger or force should color your voice or movement. Say something jolly like, "You want me to have this, Ol' Buddy? Oh, thank you so-o-o much." Wear thick gloves if you can't do this barehanded with confidence and good humor. Keep in mind that you want to create a situation where the dog willingly chooses to cease the mouthy behavior.

After hanging onto the dog's lower jaw for about a minute, gently release your grip, then quickly offer the dog your hand. Most dogs will refuse it, if for no other reason than they're not sure what's going on. Because you want to reinforce this desired behavior, gently pat and praise the dog for this response. Remember, always follow discouragement of negative behavior with an opportunity for the dog to succeed.

Car-chasing Setups

Strong evidence suggests that dogs chase cars because they are permitted to relieve themselves on both sides of the road, thereby establishing the road as territory to be protected. We can often discourage such behavior with the same technique Linda and Jim used on Yoda. Have one person drive by your house and suddenly stop the car just as your dog begins to chase it. Simultaneously, call your dog from somewhere inside your yard, enthusiastically encouraging it to come. If possible, repeat this two or three times daily until the behavior disappears. Of course, a little prevention can eliminate a lot of cure, so don't let your dog run loose to wet all over the neighborhood. Even seemingly perfectly trained dogs who never chase cars while their owners are home may chase them wildly in the owners' absence. Why? Because dogs who perceive their owners as dominant feel no need to protect the territory when their owners are home, but when the owners leave, the dogs take charge.

Relaxing a Protective Feeder

Dogs that growl threateningly at anyone who approaches them while they're eating elicit mixed responses. Some people accept this as normal dog behavior while others find it frightening. Regardless of one's view, such behavior need not exist in situations where dogs needn't protect their food from bigger, stronger members of a pack. Let's observe this problem. Four-year-old Debbie happens to be playing with her dolls on the floor near Deacon's food dish. Deacon issues a warning growl when Debbie unthinkingly moves closer to the dish. "Don't bother the dog while he's eating!" screams Debbie's mother. "No damn dog's gonna growl at my baby," roars Dad, snatching the food dish from Deacon.

For weeks, Debbie's Mom repeatedly tells Debbie to stay away from the dog while he's eating, and Dad repeatedly snatches away the dog's food dish to teach him who's boss. From this, Debbie will learn to mistrust dogs while they're eating, while Deacon will learn that Dad's the leader of the pack who wants to steal his food. In short, Dad's training technique actually increases the dog's tension. And to make matters worse, even though Debbie may never again bother Deacon while he's eating, what about her three-year-old cousin who visits occasionally? The untrained cousin could accidentally touch Deacon's dish and get a nasty bite on the hand.

To solve this problem, let the dog know that no one threatens its food. Every day, toss *more* food into your dog's dish while it's eating. Encourage visitors to do likewise. In a short time your dog will welcome people around its dish because it thinks that action means more food. You've inflicted no pain, no punishment, no power play, yet even a toddler can safely approach your dog's food dish without fear.

Grounding the Leaping Canine

When Sue Jacobs decides to tackle Willow's exuberant jumping, she invites a few friends over, warning them to wear old clothes. As people arrive, Willow jumps up to greet them, but Sue has already instructed her guests to ignore the dog completely. Because the dog jumps up to establish eye contact, every time people look at her, even to tell her to get down, they're rewarding the behavior. Without any reward, Willow soon grows bored and exhausted and wanders off to lie down. When this happens, Sue goes to the dog and quickly squats down (so there is no need for Willow to jump up) and speaks to her softly.

Depending on the age of the dog, it may take one to three weeks to cure the jumping, but it's well worth the effort. Not only will Sue have a pet that lies quietly whenever anyone enters, she also does much to relieve the tension her homecoming causes Willow.

The Weekend Pseudo-watchdog

Dog owners often initially tolerate aggressive behavior and even support it because they spend a lot of time away from home and want their dogs to protect their belongings in their absence. Owners often start this by praising a new pup every time someone rings the doorbell. "Go get 'im, Deacon!" says the owner. "Yip, yap, yap!" barks the pup. *(What the hell is that racket?)* "Atta boy, Deacon, go get him!" encourages the owner. "Yap, yap, growl, yap!" continues Deacon. *Should I stick around or get out of here? I don't know what to do. But my owner's happy, so I must be doin' good.*

The pup vocalizes its confusion while the owner reinforces the dog's fears by mistakenly praising it for what he considers protective behavior. If the owner continues doing so, the dog jumps and barks whenever anyone comes to the door, and before long the owner has to lock the dog in the basement when the doorbell rings because the dog's behavior is so distracting. How ironic: the dog that is supposed to protect its owner won't even be around whenever protection is really needed!

If your dog already exhibits such behavior, set it up. Have friends ring your bell at specific times. A few seconds before an agreed-upon arrival time, establish eye contact with your pet and tell it to sit, never taking your gaze from it until the other person rings the bell and enters the house. Then praise your pet lavishly for obeying the sit command.

If the dog gets so crazy it won't pay any attention, you'll have to devise a more creative setup. Again, have a neighbor ring the bell at a specific time. Arrange to be in the same area as your dog, not actively involved with it but standing nearby with a noisemaker (I like to use nesting metal measuring spoons which I can clasp in my palm without their making a sound). The instant the dog lunges in response to the doorbell, toss the noisemaker so it hits the floor just behind the dog. Momentarily distracted by this noise, the dog pauses, and you drop to your knees, calling the dog, making broad welcoming gestures with your arms. If the dog responds, praise it lavishly. Even if it doesn't, the distraction should give your friend ample time to enter the house without being accosted. The sudden awareness of the person already inside the house is often sufficiently disorienting to the dog to abort the excited behavior. By repeating this daily and responding consistently and with good humor, you can convert an obnoxious greeter into a pet that associates someone's arrival with a distracting and rewarding response.

The Weekend Watchdog

We'll end our discussion of training the weekend dog with a brief discussion of the best-trained dog of all, the real weekend watchdog. How does this supercanine differ from the more traditional watchdog? For one thing, unlike the dog trained purely to protect, the weekend watchdog is a happy-go-lucky, confident pet. Because of its training and self-confidence, the weekend dog trusts its owners and takes its cues from them. If the letter carrier, paperboy, and repairman don't threaten the owners, the dog pays little attention to them. On the other hand, if the owners are unsure of someone or something, the dog takes the cue from them and is on guard also.

For example, a woman who lives alone in a rather seedy neighborhood keeps her quiet, mixed-breed, spayed female denned while she's at work. She chose to den her pet after her erratic work schedule thwarted repeated efforts to control marking behavior caused by constant distracting neighborhood noises. The dog knows only two commands: sit and ready. At the command "Ready!" the dog leaps to her feet and stares right at a visitor without moving a muscle. That's all; yet the owner credits the dog with protecting her from would-be intruders on several occasions. As the woman explains it, "In this area, a well-trained dog is so rare, my dog's response to that one command gives the impression she's trained to kill!" Still, by recognizing her dog's frustrations when left alone, by choosing to den her to relieve the isolation pressure, and by taking the time and effort to train her, this weekend dog owner creates a relationship with her dog that would undoubtedly cause the dog to protect her if necessary. Because the woman taught her pet to get her cues from her owner and to have confidence in herself as well as her owner, the relationship is mutually rewarding and trouble-free. Training a weekend dog is no more difficult than training a regular dog. It just takes a little more ingenuity.

CHAPTER 8

Weekend Dog Nutrition

*C*het Poulowski used to cook an extra quarter-cup of everything he ate—soup, steak, mashed potatoes, green beans, salad, pie—for his toy fox terrier, Phoebe, until she finally got so fat she developed congestive heart failure and related digestive problems. In order to save her life, Chet now must give Phoebe daily medication and feed her a special diet that looks and tastes like wallpaper paste. The terrier finds the new diet totally distasteful and dons an expression that seems to say, *Why are you doing this to me? Why don't you love me any more?* The look in her eyes and the sight of her fat little body breaks Chet's heart. Even though he knows he shouldn't, he invariably breaks down, slipping the poor animal more table food.

When Josie Carney trained Jake, her golden retriever, she gave him a biscuit every time he did as he was told.

Yesterday he followed Josie across the busy highway in front of her home. She tried to get him to stay in the yard, but she had no biscuits. He wouldn't listen. Fortunately, the car that hit him wasn't going very fast.

Herb Crandal's been raising Old English sheepdogs for years. Back when he started, no good, balanced commercial dog foods existed, so Herb added meat, eggs, vegetable oil, vitamins, and minerals to upgrade his dogs' diet. His dogs flourished, so Herb continues the supplementation even though the commercial dog food he feeds his dogs is balanced. Jim and Pat Howard just bought one of Herb's pups, which came with three pages of feeding instructions. Because both Howards work, how can they possibly follow Herb's complex suggestions?

Veterinarians, dog owners, breeders, handlers, and trainers used to worry about unbalanced commercial dog foods, but now, thanks to regulation and a fairly conscientious industry, that's no problem. However, because most commercial dog foods are so nutritionally similar, their makers compete on the basis of such nonnutritional qualities as color, texture, and shape. Do dogs care whether their food looks like little stars or bones, is meaty red or cheesy yellow, makes its own gravy, or can be cut with a fork? Hardly. Such dog food qualities matter more to us than to our dogs.

The Normal Canine Digestive System

Before we delve into the effects our beliefs have on our dog's nutrition, let's briefly examine the canine digestive system. The dog's system works more or less like a large tube. Food goes in one end and, after reacting with enzymes from the liver, pancreas, stomach, and intestines, comes out the other in the form of waste. It's a predictable, unemotional sequence.

Given their choice, dogs tend to eat only when hungry, simply fulfilling their biological needs. Most dogs enjoying a constant supply of dry food alternate two basic feeding patterns, snacking approximately nine to eleven times daily almost every day for about three months, then snacking every two or three days for the next three months. In other words, it's normal for a dog *not* to eat every day.

In addition to a variable daily feeding schedule, dogs also naturally experience variation in nutritional needs throughout their lifetimes. The average full-grown adult dog may require half the calories a pup of the same breed and sex needs, and the geriatric canine of ten may require as little as half the calories needed by his two-year-old son and one-fourth the amount necessary to maintain his active, growing grandson. Let's take our understanding of the normal feeding pattern and changing requirements and relate them to common beliefs people hold about food and nutrition.

Beliefs Affect How
We Feed Our Dogs

The Kellermans brought home their Basset hound, Persimmon, when she was eight weeks old. Feeding her according to the directions on a popular brand of dog food, the family watched her blossom into a healthy adolescent. Once Persimmon was completely housebroken they put her on the free-choice dry food schedule recommended by their vet, allowing the dog to eat whenever she wanted. This schedule worked well. Whenever a Kellerman noticed Persimmon's bowl was empty, he or she filled it. Sometimes the children, Jeremy and Liz, filled it after school.

Other times their parents, Hank and Ellen, did it before going to work.

Although the Kellermans planned to breed their dog, they were seldom home, so when Persimmon turned nine months old, off she went to the vet's to be spayed. When she returned home forty-eight hours later, the whole family fussed over her, keeping close watch on her stitches and her diet. The dog looked and acted fine, but the Kellermans suddenly realized she wasn't eating as much as she used to.

Seeing Persimmon's half-full food dish, Jeremy Kellerman insists, "She's tired of that dry stuff!"

"Let's give her some canned food, like Lassie eats," pipes up Liz.

"Do you think she's sick, Hon?" Hank Kellerman asks his wife.

"I don't know," replies Ellen. "Let's see if she'll eat this leftover roast beef and gravy."

Persimmon's problem is not a problem at all, but rather the natural result of maturation. Her appetite gradually decreased over a period of months in response to the decreased nutritional needs accompanying normal maturation, but the Kellermans missed this because the dog is a self-feeder. As long as Persimmon acted fine, no one worried about how often her dish was being filled or by whom. However, when Persimmon leaves the house for surgery, then returns two days later, the family becomes acutely aware of her habits. To them, the Basset's decline in appetite seems quite sudden, and therefore undoubtedly related to her surgery. To make matters worse, the Kellermans, like many people, associate regular feeding with health. To be sure, loss of appetite often signals illness, but remember that it is normal for a dog *not* to eat periodically. A consistent refusal to eat should cause concern, but how the dog looks and acts is more important than how much it eats.

Dogs Learn from What and When We Feed Them

When Liz and Jeremy slip Persimmon part of their peanut butter sandwiches or when their mother mixes roast beef and gravy with the dog's food, they teach the dog three things:

* To eat for taste rather than nutritional need.
* That food equals love.
* That she need only ignore her food to generate a dietary change.

Let's look closely at each of these lessons. What tastes good to dogs? Most people would answer steak, bones, or meaty-flavored canned dog food. But a lot of dogs might actually prefer frozen cow flops, old deer carcasses, and squashed squirrels. Yet because people supply the food, our own taste preferences tend to dictate what we feed our dogs. If Jeremy Kellerman loves his after-school peanut butter snack and shares it with his dog while he tells her about his day, Persimmon quickly develops a fondness for peanut butter. If Ellen forgets to fill Persimmon's bowl because she has a deadline to meet but shares her midafternoon cheese and crackers to make up for the oversight, the dog will undoubtedly appear at her side that time each afternoon. In both cases, human preferences or guilt have colored the normal eating process, and Persimmon couples her natural desire to be with her people with food.

Whether they own dogs or not, many people perceive food as a token of love or acceptance. Persimmon's madly thumping tail and happy grin when she sees a peanut butter sandwich or smells cheese or roast beef have little to do with her nutritional needs. Although we may argue whether Persimmon prefers roast beef or peanut butter to raw rabbits or wild birds, her reaction to food relates directly to their source, her owners. If we ask the Kellermans to describe their dog's ideal diet, they will probably name the popular brand of dog food she has available at all times, rather than peanut butter sandwiches or even roast beef. Though they recognize a nutritionally sound diet for their dog, that doesn't prevent them from supplementing that diet with something that suits their *tastes* rather than Persimmon's *needs*.

Let's go back seven months to when Persimmon was a pup. From the very first day she rushes to greet anyone who enters the Kellerman house, wiggling all over, thumping her tail joyfully. As part of their after-school ritual, Jeremy and Liz prepare a snack which they share with their pet. Soon they begin training her to sit and lie down, using food treats as rewards whenever Persimmon obeys. In a very short time the Basset's spontaneous tail-wagging and eagerness to be with and please her people becomes related to food; and if food doesn't appear, she's unhappy. In other words, the Kellermans use Persimmon's spontaneous offerings of love and companionship to *train* her to bestow them in response to food.

Now let's see what happens when Persimmon returns from the vet. A subtle but definite change occurs: their dog acts happy (loved) but she's not eating. Because the Kellermans believe health and well-being depend on food intake, they think something's wrong. Their own human tastes and food-equals-love belief now create a *negative* reaction to a *normal* dietary decrease. Because food has become such an integral part of the family's relationship with Persimmon, the Kellermans are likely to react to any change in her behavior with a food change, rather than the *belief* change necessary to restore a natural relationship with their pet.

How and Why We Feed Our Dogs Affects What We Feed Them

Dogs, like many animals, are a conditioned-response species. This means that if we reward certain behavior, the dog tends to repeat that behavior. What does that have to do with Persimmon's not eating? A great deal. Suppose we start a young pup on some dull but balanced dry food with no emotional attachments. As the pup approaches maturity, it gradually decreases its food intake to coincide with decreasing biological needs. But suppose every time the pup skips a meal, we embellish or change the food. If this change parallels the dog's first decline in nutritional needs at around six months of age, a smart dog can soon dismiss so many commercial dog foods that by the time it is a year old its owners will believe it will eat nothing but table food.

A devious dog? No, just a normal dog making the conditioned response characteristic of the species. Every time owners change food, they actually reward their dogs for *not* eating while simultaneously teasing the dogs to eat beyond their biological needs. This not only leads to dietary imbalance, but often to overweight. And nothing baffles the contemporary dog owner more than a fat dog. Much of our weekend culture today centers around physical fitness and good health; we have to be fit and healthy just to maintain the pace. But what about our sleek black Lab pup, appropriately named Arrow, who starts to resemble a bowling ball five years later? While teasing a child to overeat with ice cream and candy treats would horrify most people, adding meat or gravy to a dog's food doesn't. That's because many of our reasons for feeding our dogs are often far different from our reasons for feeding ourselves or our children. Many of us attach much more emotion to our pets' food than we do to our own.

Too often, guilt rather than logic determines the kinds or amount of food we give our pets. I don't mean to imply that weekend dog owners don't know or care about nutrition. They do. In fact, weekend dog owners usually display greater sensitivity to the physical needs of their pets than many traditional dog owners; but that very sensitivity usually comes from guilty feelings about not being home enough. When your mother-in-law insinuates that you don't love your dog because it has a lean look, you feel personally attacked. But it's not necessary to defend yourself. The only thing that counts is how *you* feel about how much and what your dog eats.

Too Much Fat or Not Enough?

Are *you* happy with how your dog looks and acts? How do you evaluate *good* from a nutritional standpoint? To answer that question, you must stand back to get an overall feel for your pet. Watch how it moves. Is its coat shiny and smooth? Eyes bright and alert? Does it respond to its surroundings? To be sure, these are subjective questions whose answers depend on an animal's age and breed. On the other hand, most dog owners seem to know intuitively how their dogs look and act when they're healthy. Unfortunately, because of the emotions associated with it, weight alone can mislead us. Even owners who have no difficulty assessing their dogs' general health may have problems being objective about weight.

To assess weight, *lightly* place both hands, palms down, on your dog's rib cage. Make sure your hands are over the chest and not the abdomen (stomach). Roundness or fullness in the stomach area tells more about gas than fat. Some very thin dogs display distended abdomens and some normal ones appear thin in this area. With your hands properly placed, you should be able to feel bone but not be able to easily count ribs. On the other hand, you should not have to probe deeply to detect ribs, either. With a little practice, you'll learn to distinguish fur from fat. Although full-coated breeds such as collies, huskies, and Keeshonds may appear rotund, careful palpation will usually reveal the amount of fat under all that hair.

If you're still not sure whether your dog has too much

or too little fat, ask another person to conduct this test for you. Your veterinarian may spring to mind, but the vet may or may not prove helpful. For example, some people in my area believe I like dogs too thin while I'm equally convinced they like dogs too fat. Still, if Susie, the poodle, strikes me as being two pounds overweight, but it causes her no physiological problems and her owner likes her that way, that's okay. But if Susie's weight bothers either her or her owner, that's not okay, and a change may be in order.

Once you're satisfied with your dog's weight, keeping a simple record will help you maintain that weight.

Dog's Name *Susie*

Date	Weight	Amount Fed
4/8/80	16 lbs.	3/4 cup dry food, 4 biscuits per day
10/8/80	18 lbs.	Decrease to 1/2 cup dry, 2 biscuits per day
12/8/80	17 lbs.	Decrease to 1/2 cup dry, no biscuits
4/8/82	16 lbs.	1/2 cup dry, no treats
10/8/83	16 lbs.	1/2 cup dry, no treats
4/8/84	16 lbs.	1/2 cup dry, no treats

As the chart shows, a dog's weight may vary, so you may need to adjust the amount you feed occasionally. Dogs with weight problems should be weighed frequently to keep track of their progress. For dogs that eat the same balanced diet all the time on a free-choice feeding schedule with no snacks, semiannual weight checks usually suffice.

A personalized chart makes more sense than breed standards or even the feeding charts one sees on dog food packages. Each dog's nutritional needs may vary according to age, sex, and life-style. Although weighing your dog and tailoring its diet to its needs may seem time-consuming, such a habit can prevent the gradual weight gain or loss busy weekend dog owners often overlook until the problem becomes obvious and serious. Trying to get weight off an obese dog or weight on one with digestive problems consumes much more time than periodic canine weigh-ins. If you can lift your dog, weigh yourself holding it on a bathroom scale. By subtracting your weight from the combined weight, you'll find your dog's weight. If you can't lift your dog, a local feed store will probably let you use their scales, or your veterinarian can weigh your pet for you.

Determining Nutritional Norms

All this talk about beliefs may give you the feeling that there are no fixed standards regarding pet nutrition. To some extent that's true. Fat, like beauty, can be in the eye of the beholder. Nevertheless, useful nutrition guidelines do exist. Remember the digestive tube? What comes out can tell us a great deal about the appropriateness of what went in. The amount and consistency of your dog's stool can signal digestive problems that may require veterinary care; is it too hard, semiformed, watery? Then take the dog to your vet for a checkup.

Although one of the characteristics of a good weekend dog owner is a willingness to change, that only applies when *change is necessary*. Owners of new dogs often forget it may take a dog a week or more to adjust to a new environment, and a dog's food intake may decrease dramatically during this time. The new dog may even be a so-called easy keeper, one that requires minimum food to maintain optimum weight. Rather than compare your dog's food intake to someone else's, get a feeling for what's normal for your particular dog.

Because dogs are territorial—that is, have a strong sense of place—major environmental changes such as a new home or owner can produce great stress. In a new environment problems such as parasites, borderline digestive irregularities, or viruses may suddenly flare up and require immediate medical attention.

Never wait until your dog gets sick to examine it. Look at it now. Notice how much and how often it eats. Is the dog a cyclic feeder, snacking almost daily for three months, then eating every second to third day for the next three? Or does it feed seasonally, preferring to crunch away at 5 A.M. during the hot summer months but at 5 P.M. during the winter? Many weekend owners discover that their dogs eat only when they're home, even if food is always available. If protecting territory preoccupies a dog during its owner's absence, it has neither the time nor the inclination to eat until the owner returns. However, once the owner does come home, it dives right it.

Averting Nutritional Problems by Changing Beliefs

One particular human belief about dogs poses one of the biggest threats to weekend nutrition—the belief that they need meat. Of course wild dogs eat meat, but when we toss a weekend dog a hunk of raw beef or a knuckle bone with the idea that this is what our pet would normally or naturally be eating, we're dead wrong. Wild dogs do not eat just muscle meat and gnaw on bones; they consume the entire prey. Because carnivores tend to prey on plant-eating herbivores, a wild dog's diet often includes several feet of vegetation-packed intestine. Whereas whole rabbits may very well provide a balanced meal, a chunk of rabbit thigh bone and muscle does not.

Furthermore, raw meat does not offer a particularly efficient source of protein and other nutrients for a domesticated dog whose breeding has produced a less vigorous

digestive tract than its wild cousins'. As a dog ages, its
digestive organs function less well than they did in the
past, but raw meat demands maximum digestion. Wild
dogs suffer from this problem less than domesticated ones
because pack competition and the rigors of outdoor life
result in shorter life-spans. Furthermore, the digestive system is a highly specialized one and the more highly specialized a tissue or organ, the less likely it is to repair itself
with *functional* tissue as it wears out. Thus a pancreas that
has to produce maximum enzymes to digest a demanding
diet eventually loses the ability to produce those enzymes.
Then the owner must decide whether he or she can prepare special diets and/or provide supplementary enzymes
daily. Such treatment requires close monitoring, which
many weekend owners often have neither the time nor the
financial wherewithal to pursue.

Before trying to solve any food-related problem, review
the five most common nutritional beliefs that get weekend
dog owners into trouble:

• Food equals love.
• Dogs like to eat what people like to eat.
• All dogs have the same nutritional needs and patterns
  for their entire lives.
• Dogs won't like us, or learn, if we don't give them
  treats.
• Fat or skinny dogs are sick.

Our dogs' nutritional needs parallel neither those of
wild animals nor those of fur-coated little people, but they
do reflect the needs of a companion species. Simple and
self-regulating, their systems require little beyond owner
awareness of what is normal and healthy for each individual.

CHAPTER 9

Solving Food-related Problems

*P*olly, the obese poodle, sniffs the bowl of dry kibble that replaces her usual bowl of tasty people food one evening.

"That's it, Polly. The vet says you're too fat and I'm killing you with food." Owner Dan Taft watches Polly settle her pudgy little body next to her food bowl; she stares at him forlornly. "Stop looking at me like that!"

In spite of all the extra treats the Boyntons feed their Malamute, Mukluk, he never seems to gain any weight. Although he's extremely active, cavorting with other dogs and charging all over the neighborhood while his owners are at work, he looks so thin it's becoming embarrassing.

Susie Holman co-owns a natural foods store and wants only the best, most natural foods for herself and her German shepherd pup, Shiloh. She heavily supplements Shiloh's commercial dog food with vitamins, minerals, and alfalfa. Still the pup isn't growing well and exhibits nonspecific medical problems such as lethargy, whining, and intermittent lameness.

The solutions to common weekend dog nutritional problems begin with an understanding of *how* the problem occurred. Our dogs' actions, how they look, and how we feel about it may tell us something's wrong, but before we attack any food-related problem we must ask ourselves three key questions:

1. Is it a people problem? How do *I* feel about the quality and quantity of food I feed my dog and how it looks?
2. Is it a dog problem? Is my dog willing to eat or able to utilize what I feed it?
3. Is it a food problem? Am I feeding my dog the right amount of the right food?

If we can't honestly classify a problem within one or more of these categories, then no problem may exist. Nutritional problems such as overweight or underweight are *not* problems if they don't bother either you or your dog. If I, as your veterinarian and friend, give your dog a clean bill of health but say your pet is too fat, too thin, or on a poor-quality diet, only you can decide whether you agree. Don't create a problem if you don't believe one exists. Always balance your willingness to change with the confidence that you know what's right for you and your dog.

Is It a People Problem?
Changing Food-related Beliefs

Solving food-related problems may require that we change our beliefs about food, then make the necessary dietary changes for our dogs to reflect those beliefs. This may mean, for example, that we must replace our own emphasis on our dogs' food with affection and activity in our dogs' lives. Before attacking a food-related problem, ask yourself these questions:

- How do I feel about the problem?
- What consequences will the existing diet inflict on my dog's health and happiness? On my own?
- How do I feel about changing my dog's diet?
- Do my schedule and life-style permit a dietary change?
- Is it worth it?

Unless you believe that changing your dog's diet is the right thing for *both* of you, any dietary change will fail. We can whittle off pounds by simply not feeding the dog. That's no problem. We can add pounds by feeding more or different foods. We can stop oversupplementation. But how we feel about what we're feeding our dogs can plunge us back onto the roller-coaster guilt trip that traps even the most loving, knowledgeable, well-meaning owner.

Although I don't recommend fasting as a means of weight reduction for dogs, scientists using such methods have obtained some interesting results that can benefit weekend dog owners. First of all, they noted that hospitalized dogs can last for extended periods of time provided they receive affection and activity, especially during those periods when the dog would normally be eating. Second, dogs that achieve optimal weight within such closely monitored programs often regain weight as soon as they return to their owners. Even an overweight dog forgets about food if it sees something better to do. Think about that. If there's an exciting program on TV, or we're involved in a good book or fun project, we forget all about eating, too. The fact that a dog regains weight when it returns home tells us that continual optimal weight depends on changes in the owners and the households. Underweight dogs also create special belief problems for their owners. If we're not home and have a skinny dog, people may say it's because we don't have the time to feed the dog properly.

Is It a Dog Problem?

If you think your dog is too skinny, too fat, or doesn't utilize its food well, ask yourself:

- How does the dog look? Use the rib test. Has it always been like this or did it happen recently?
- How does the dog act?
- Has the dog's food or feeding schedule changed?
- How does the stool (bowel movement) look?

If the dog looks and acts normal and its stool is within normal limits, the problem may be yours rather than the dog's. However, if either your dog or its stool looks abnormal, there may be a medical problem. If you have any doubts, take your dog to your vet.

What Is Normal Stool?

The color and consistency of a dog's stool can tell us a lot about what's going on in the digestive tube. Much of what the dog eats affects the color of its stool. A highly dyed red food will color it red. Such coloration is not necessarily bad, provided the dog is otherwise healthy. However, if the dog appears unhealthy or if the color of the stool changes when the diet has not, the dog should be examined. Dark-brown to black, orangish-yellow, or gray-colored stool can signal serious digestive problems. Here again, it's important you know what's normal for your dog. This may be quite difficult to determine if you feed all kinds of food or if your dog runs loose while you're at work and you've no idea what it eats when you're gone.

The consistency of the stool can also tell you a lot about what's going on inside that digestive tube. You can pick up normal-consistency stool with a paper towel without leaving a mark; otherwise it's too soft. If it appears tarry, watery, or comes out in rock-hard little balls, the dog's having problems and should be examined.

Many people are unaware of the color and consistency of their dog's stool because they don't want to look at it. That's unfortunate, and can get the weekend dog owner and dog into a lot of trouble. For example, suppose Don Boynton's washing the dinner dishes and looking out the kitchen window one evening after work. In the backyard he notices Mukluk crouch and strain, then move a little, then crouch and strain again. Is Mukluk constipated? Should Don give the dog some oil to loosen him up? Don should know that very few things cause constipation in dogs; *the most common cause of straining in the dog is diarrhea*. If Don assumes his dog's constipated because he doesn't want to take the time to go outside and actually check what Mukluk's producing or because he finds examining stool distasteful, he could wind up making the problem much worse by misdiagnosing and mistreating it.

Constipation: Make No Bones About It

Bones are about the only nutritional cause of hard stool (constipation) in dogs. After giving enemas to numerous dogs impacted with rock hard stool filled with needlesharp bone fragments, I'm convinced that bones are much more trouble than they're worth. All bones. Not just chicken and pork bones. All bones. Get your dog a hard nylon bone substitute instead. It may not be as tasty and the Boyntons may have to train Mukluk to use it, but it's well worth the effort. Rubbing the nylon bone with your hands or putting it in the dirty laundry basket for a few days will impart a scent most dogs find attractive. As a last-ditch effort, you can rub it with a piece of meat or cheese, but beware that you're perpetuating the food-is-something-other-than-nutrition belief.

False Constipation: A Hairy Matter

Another common cause of straining, especially in shaggy poodles, poodle mixes, sheepdogs, and other breeds with long, silky coats (Yorkies, Lhasas) is false constipation. When this occurs, stool gets caught in the fur around the rectum and the dog can't get it off. Some of these animals may strain to the point of creating diarrhea as well as making the area quite sore and inflamed. Assuming the dog is constipated and giving it oil only makes the condition worse. To detect false constipation, all you have to do is look at the area under the tail. If it's covered with fecal material, simply cleanse the area repeatedly with warm water and a mild soap. Keeping the hair clipped short in this area helps eliminate the problem.

Parasites

With any suspected digestive problem, it's always a good idea to have the stool checked even if it looks essentially normal. Intestinal parasites are one of the most common and most easily rectified causes of weight loss and decreased food utilization in dogs. They can be particularly serious in young pups and geriatric animals. You can check your pet's stool for the spaghetti like roundworms, but if you don't see them, don't assume your dog doesn't have worms.

Often only the mature worms or microscopic eggs are passed in the stool, and the animal may be loaded with immature worms and show no worms in the stool at all. Or the dog may have hookworms or whipworms, both of which are so tiny you may not see them in the stool. These two worms can do more damage than the larger roundworms, because in addition to soaking up nutrients meant for the dog, they attach to the animal's intestine and cause irritation. In my experience, animals with worm problems, especially hookworms, have much more difficulty with intestinal viruses, such as Parvo. The stress caused by the parasites as well as their effects on the animal's nutritional status and intestinal lining undoubtedly hinder its ability to fight off a tough gastrointestinal infection.

The best way to make sure your dog doesn't have intestinal parasites is to take a fresh stool sample to your vet for a thorough microscopic examination. Be sure to mention anything unusual you notice in the stool. Veterinarians will usually check the sample for eggs, but if the dog has immature worms that are not reproducing, or if it has tapeworms, which normally don't reproduce by laying eggs, the sample may be falsely negative. This doesn't mean that such tests are useless; it does mean that to get the most out of any test, you must provide all the information you can. Other tests beside the routine worm checks may reveal unusual problems. Weekend dog owners who run out some dark August night and scoop up some stool with a plastic bag, toss it into the trunk of the car, then drop it off at the vet's on the way home from work a week later aren't getting their money's worth. When you walk your dog or clean up the yard, look at the stool. Get a feel for normal and abnormal. When you take a sample, take a fresh one. If you're pressed for time, write a brief note to the vet or technician telling him or her what you're seeing. To be sure, collecting stool samples and dropping them off at the vet's is no one's idea of a good time. So do it right the first time.

Too Much Stool

If the stool appears normal but there seems to be too much of it, your dog may be unable to process its diet. A lot of dogs simply can't handle certain commercial dog foods. In general, these dogs will eat well and some are so active, their owners use the term "hyperactive" to describe them. In addition to acting wired up and producing frequent and/or large amounts of seemingly normal stool, many also emit lots of gas. Dogs don't burp as easily as

people so most gas exits from the rear. Although a dog
may periodically produce semiformed or watery stools,
the owner most often notices the amount. As one client
aptly says, "It's three cups of food in and two cups of stool
out!"

If your dog's one of these mammoth stool producers
who's acting fine otherwise, you may want to try a few dietary changes. First, eliminate all foods other than the dog
food. The more varied the menu, the more difficult to
identify any nutritional culprit. Sometimes simply eliminating more irritating snacks and dog treats solves the problem. If not, offer the dog food in three or four smaller
meals. Often a dog can handle irritating or relatively indigestible foods in smaller amounts. Not only does the digestive tract resemble a tube, it also functions as a conveyer
belt. If we put three cups of food in and the system can
only digest one properly, the remaining two cups will
come off the belt more or less undigested. If the food is
irritating as well as indigestible, the system speeds up to
get rid of the irritant. Because the amount of water the
dog's system absorbs from the food parallels the amount
of time the food is in the digestive tract, speeding this
transit time may result in less water absorption. The result,
diarrhea!

If multiple feedings don't help or if you can't fit them
into your schedule, try sprinkling unseasoned meat tenderizer on the food. The main ingredient in most of these
products is papain, a natural enzyme from the papaya
plant. It functions by assisting the body's natural digestive
enzymes in the breakdown of the food. Sometimes this
digestive assistance is all the dog needs to enable it to handle an otherwise troublesome diet.

Finally, you might consider changing the diet altogether.
For a dog with any kind of digestive problem, I recommend doing this very gradually. Sometimes food A or food
B won't irritate the system, but the *change* from A to B totally upsets it. The best switch from an irritating diet is rice

flavored with a *small* amount of chicken. I emphasize a small amount because meat and meat by-products require maximum digestive function and many domestic dogs have lost this capacity. A gentle diet of rice flavored with a small amount of chicken will usually soothe an irritated digestive system in forty-eight to seventy-two hours.

Solving Digestive Problems
(Too much stool, too many bowel movements, gassiness)

Step 1. Eliminate all dog treats and table food. Feed only commercial dry dog food free choice. If this doesn't help, go to step 2.

Step 2. Sprinkle food liberally with unseasoned meat tenderizer. If dog responds, gradually decrease the amount of tenderizer to the lowest level to control the problem. If this doesn't work, go to step 3.

Step 3. Gradually switch diet to one of the high-quality dry products available from most vets. If this doesn't work, go to step 4.

Step 4. Switch to a canned food and feed three or four times daily if schedule permits, twice daily if it doesn't. Avoid all-meat and/or meat by-product foods. If this doesn't help, go to step 5.

Step 5. Feed special commercial canned food designed for older dogs. Feed small amounts three or four times daily if possible, at least twice daily if not. If this doesn't work, see step 6.

Step 6. Have dog thoroughly examined. This may include repeated stool samples, blood work, and/or X rays.

Regardless of the change, always initiate the new food or schedule over a period of at least four days, replacing one-quarter of the old diet with the new each day. If diarrhea, vomiting, gas, or discomfort occurs at any point, return to the preceding day's schedule and follow that combination for one or two more days. Here again, multiple small feedings seem to work better, if you can fit them into your schedule.

Feeding Schedule to Introduce New Diet

Day One	3/4 old diet mixed with 1/4 new
Day Two	1/2 old diet, 1/2 new
Day Three	3/4 new diet, 1/4 old
Day Four	All new diet

What commercial food should you use? That's a hard question. A gurgling digestive tract producing gassy, giant stool may come from three major sources: incomplete protein digestion, incomplete carbohydrate digestion, or irritating dyes and/or preservatives. In general, I prefer to keep a dog on dry food if possible because a balanced dry food tends to be nutritional and relatively palatable. Dogs fed dry food with no interfering owner beliefs or dog beliefs (such as competitive eating between two dogs in one household) will usually snack and eat only to fulfill biological needs. As far as *which* commercial dry food, I tend to prefer the least dyed and most unimaginatively shaped ones. Lately I've found the diets available from veterinarians and professionals, such as Hill's Prescription and Science diets, Iames, and Eukanuba, well worth the extra cost for dogs with digestive problems. In addition to being well balanced, these diets contain few of the additives and nonnutritional "fill" associated with the production of owner-pleasing commercial dog foods. Consequently, the average dog eats about half as much of these foods, producing half the stool. By the time you figure out how much you're spending for regular dog food, stool checks, and veterinary exams for the problem feeder, plus the time involved in cleaning up the yard, such foods can be quite a bargain.

Warning: Never switch a dog with digestive problems to one of the so-called high-protein dog foods without consulting your veterinarian. These foods contain a lot of protein, but it's often poor-*quality* protein which can wreck havoc in a sensitive system. Also, even if the dog doesn't *need* all that protein, the digestive system still has to digest it as best it can.

If the dog still does not gain weight or continues producing large amounts of stool compared to the amount of food eaten, you may want to switch gradually to a good-quality canned food. Canned food contains much less crude fiber (crude carbohydrate) than dry food and often helps those dogs that can't handle large amounts of fiber in their diets. When switching to a canned product, use the one-quarter per day replacement technique and stay away from all-meat and meat by-product canned foods, which tend to be more difficult for dogs to digest. I'm particularly pleased with Cycle 4 chicken dog food, a chicken-based canned food designed for older dogs. Many older animals, those with digestive problems and those that are allergic to beef, can easily handle this food containing relatively little fat or fiber and a good-quality protein.

Is It a Feeding Problem?

Slimming Down the Overweight Dog

If your dog appears physically fit except for its weight, the problem is probably a food one, a matter of how much and what you feed your dog. Begin by getting a good feel for just how much and what the dog eats. Many times, people supply the right amount and kind of dog food but extra treats put on the weight. For example, one tablespoon of vegetable oil or animal fat has about the same number

of calories as a fifteen-ounce can of some dog foods. When
we start adding meat scraps (which usually contain too
much fat for our own tastes) to the dog's food, the dog can
pick up quite a few calories. What might seem like a
smidgen of ice cream or gravy to a 140-pound adult human can be quite a load for a 5-pound poodle. Keep track
of all food intake, listing every bite for a week before you
consider any changes. Measure carefully. Don't put down
"a little popcorn" but "1/2 cup." This simple chart should
help:

	MORNING	AFTERNOON	EVENING
MONDAY	½ cup dry food ¼ piece toast	2 small pieces cheese 1 pretzel	½ cup dry food, 5 cheese puffs, 5 pieces beef, ½ ginger cookie, 3 tbsp. gravy
TUESDAY			
WEDNESDAY			
THURSDAY			
FRIDAY			
SATURDAY			
SUNDAY			

Fortunately, overweight dogs can lose weight quickly once food changes are initiated. A fifty-pound dog that should weigh forty can lose up to two pounds a week without any adverse effects. However, weight-loss goals should reflect the breed's ideal size and your own feelings.

Decreasing the food intake may be done several ways. If the dog is on a balanced diet but is getting too much, the owner can simply decrease the amount being fed. If the dog is normally fed only once a day, dividing the smaller amount of food into two or three meals is often beneficial. I prefer this approach because it increases owner interaction with the dog while decreasing the amount of food; thus love and companionship replace food, reestablishing the natural relationship with the dog.

An overweight dog that's a begger may be kept outdoors while the family eats and until all leftovers are out of sight. If that seems too coldhearted, keep a small bowl of shredded lettuce or dry dog food on the dining table next to you. When your dog begs, offer it lettuce or kibble. If it accepts, it is getting low-caloried or balanced fare. If it refuses, it has chosen to give up the begging itself.

If you have been adding table food to your dog's kibble as well as feeding it from the table, this practice will have to cease if it is to regain its healthful weight and a balanced nutritional status. Stopping all table food cold turkey works, but it can also cause both dog and owner emotional trauma. It's better to use a gradual approach, replacing one-quarter the existing diet with the new one weekly, over about a month's time. How long it takes to accomplish the desired weight loss matters less than creating the necessary changes in beliefs and diet to maintain that optimum weight.

The Bantamweight Weekend Dog

In addition to parasites and/or an inability to digest certain types of food, another common cause of underweight is simply not feeding the dog enough. If the dog looks and acts fine but is too thin, give it more food. Here again, free choice or multiple feedings work best. Young dogs, like Mukluk, that have just too many other exciting things to do besides eat, can fall prey to this problem and often normal maturation processes resolve it. Never tease an otherwise normal dog with special treats or dietary embellishments or you'll wind up with a problem feeder that's not only thin but also eating an unbalanced diet. Simply offer more of the regular dog food.

The Boyntons may also want to consider keeping Mukluk home during their absence. Whenever attacking any nutritional problem, it makes things much easier if we eliminate as many variables as possible. If Mukluk gets the correct amount and kind of food for a house dog but he's off running all day plus eating Lord-knows-what at the landfill, the Boyntons may find any dietary changes unsuccessful. Remember, regardless of where your dog goes in your absence and what it eats, only you are responsible for your dog and its diet. If you have no idea where it is and what it's doing or eating when you're gone, you'll have no way of knowing what, if anything, to change.

Oversupplementation

Many veterinarians believe that oversupplementation rivals overweight as the number-one nutritional problem in dogs today. Much of this comes from our weekend society. We're physically fit and health conscious. We are, like Susie Holman, down on junk food and additives, high on natural products. And because we love our dogs, we want the best for them, too. But it always goes back to the same thing: what's good for us may not necessarily be good for our dogs. We already know that the majority of dog foods on the market today are balanced; therefore, anything we add is excessive. If we add a teaspoon of calcium or B vitamins to a dog's food and the dog doesn't need it, it may excrete it, but not before the substance exerts its effect. In a growing pup like Shiloh, the correct and delicate ratios of calcium, phosphorus, and vitamin D, to name a few, are critical for normal growth and bone development. When Susie quadruples the amount of calcium in Shiloh's diet, a nutritional and metabolic chain reaction occurs affecting the levels of these and other vitamins and minerals. And in order for all those unneeded water-soluble B vitamins to show up in her urine, Shiloh's urinary system must work harder. To be sure, the digestive system works like a tube, but everything that goes into the system must be handled, whether the dog derives any benefit from it or not. And the system, like all living things, can only handle so much. What taxes the digestive system, taxes the circulatory system, the respiratory system, and the excretory system. In short, if we overload one system, we overload them all.

It doesn't bother me if Susie wants to start from scratch and cook a special, balanced, all-natural diet for Shiloh that meets the dog's needs. That's fine. What does bother me is when owners supplement the dog's diet to fulfill their needs rather than the dog's. If your dog is on any of the commonly available dog foods, the chances are extremely slim that *any* supplementation is necessary if your dog is looking and acting well. If it isn't, if its coat seems dry and dull, the amount and consistency of its stool is abnormal, or it appears reluctant to eat the diet, consult your veterinarian. It's far more likely he or she may recommend a *total* dietary change. Keep in mind that we weekend dog owners often supplement our pets' diets because we're looking for ways to make up for those hours we're away from home, rather than because we're responding to any real nutritional need of the dog.

Monitoring the Problem Dog and Owner

Once we establish the reason for the food-related problem and initiate the necessary changes to correct it, we must monitor the dog and ourselves carefully. Owners plagued by guilt regarding their skinny dogs are often so pleased with a weight gain that they can soon find themselves with a fat dog on their hands. Dogs with digestive problems switched to more appropriate diets or feeding schedules may actually gain weight on the same or even a lesser amount of food. Runners that are kept home may suddenly blossom into pudginess. Owners of obese dogs that achieve their optimum weight after dieting may suddenly be tempted to reward the dog's weight loss with a few extra treats.

Once you establish a workable type and amount of food as well as an effective feeding schedule and life-style for yourself and your dog, *stick with it.* Although you could begin gradually introducing treats and supplements or change the feeding schedule, why rock the boat? That piece-of-steak love offering may cause your dog forty-eight hours of digestive discomfort. Is that love? Even though it's medically possible to reintroduce such foods, why do it if you truly believe that your pet's affection has nothing to do with what it eats? When Polly becomes accustomed to her all-dog food diet in a healthful amount, why would Dan *want* to begin offering her tidbits from the table again? If Shiloh's unsupplemented diet results in a strong, healthy pet, who cares how great the algae-wheat germ capsules have been for Susie's partner's dog? And if the Boyntons know Mukluk gets into junk and burns up more calories than he takes in during his daily romps, is letting him run loose an act of love? Always remember: people who believe their love for their dog and their dog's love for them is a mutually rewarding bond do not feel guilty or unhappy making any changes necessary to maintain their pet's health.

Put down the bone meal; put down the steak; put down the Twinkies and the kelp. Pick up the dog and hug it instead.

To summarize, remember these nutritional principles:

- Weekend dog nutritional problems arise from three different sources: (a) how we feel about what the dog eats, (b) how the dog utilizes what it eats, and (c) what and how much we feed the dog.
- A dog's nutritional needs depend on age, breed, sex, heredity, and environmental factors.
- A dog's nutritional status and needs should be evaluated in terms of how it looks and feels rather than how much and what it eats.
- An owner cannot successfully initiate a change in a dog's nutritional status unless he or she believes it's the right thing for both of them.
- Solutions to food-related problems work best if you tailor them to both your needs and your dog's.

CHAPTER 10

The Total Weekend Dog Workout Program

*T*hree-year-old Trinket has free access to Adele Metzger's large sunny yard at the end of a secluded dirt road, but the shy little Pomeranian never goes more than thirty feet from the patio. Between her busy schedule and a troublesome hip, Adele finds it difficult to routinely exercise the dog, although she's concerned about Trinket's tendency to gain weight.

Mukluk, the Boyntons' Malamute, loves to fetch sticks outdoors. Unless his owners provide long daily exercise sessions before they leave for work, Mukluk gets bored and damages the house while they're gone. The Boyntons dread bad weather, which restricts their play sessions.

Steve and Joanie Bennet are planning a two-week hiking and camping trip in June, so in January they begin to work out at the local fitness center each noon. In April, they begin jogging three miles after work each evening. Although they'll take Colonel, their shepherd, on the trip, he's actually been getting less exercise lately because the Bennets don't like to jog with the dog.

Although every dog requires exercise based on its age, breed, sex, and temperament, each owner must decide how to fulfill this need. If Adele Metzger gave up regular workouts years ago, she may not encourage Trinket to do anything more than the minimum. On the other hand, often owners of active dogs like Mukluk find they must build an active workout program for their pet or face mighty consequences.

Owners tend to believe that the larger the dog, the more exercise it needs. Furthermore, they think the larger the dog, the more room it requires for exercise. To be sure, a dog's size affects its exercise needs, as we will see shortly, *but an owner can meet those needs fully, even for a 150-pound Great Pyrenees, in a two-bedroom apartment*. All it takes is a little imagination.

Before we learn how to exploit limited exercise space, we must determine whether we and our dogs want to exercise at all. In theory all animals, including humans, should exercise daily to maintain good health. However, we all know people who shrink from any form of regular physical activity as if it were a terminal disease. And although medical testing may show that these nonexercising individuals have less healthy muscle tone, reflexes, or heart rate, we would find it hard to separate exercisers from nonexercisers solely on the basis of appearance. Does lack of exercise itself cause overweight? No. Overweight results from overeating, not underexercising. If one dog's daily exercise burns up 500 more calories than its sedentary littermate's, the exercising animal can consume 500 more calories and still maintain its optimum weight.

However, if the sedentary animal consumes the same number of calories as its more active friend, it's going to get fat. By the same token, the exerciser cannot reduce its workout program without proportionally limiting its food intake or it will get fat, too.

Determining Your Dog's Exercise Needs

How do you determine a dog's exercise needs? Begin by carefully observing your dog within your normal routine. Does the animal ever appear hyper or agitated, as though looking for something to do? Do you have to coax it to fetch a tossed ball? Does your dog leap into the air every time you say, "Want to go out?" or "Want to play ball?" Or does it slowly open one eye, then the other, stretch, and look at you with yawning indifference?

Once we've established how our dogs feel about exercise, we must evaluate our own feelings about it. If the dog is a real sluggard but its owner is gung ho about rigorous daily workouts, or if the dog craves constant activity while the owner prefers to sit in front of the television set, relationships will suffer unless something changes. Remember our options?

- Accept the situation as it exists, including how we feel about it.
- Change the way we feel about it.
- Change the dog to align it with our beliefs.
- Get rid of the dog.

Of course, mismatched owner/dog pairs can enjoy good relationships, provided the active owner doesn't resent the dog's inactivity and the sedentary owner doesn't feel guilty about not exercising the active dog. However, if the owner experiences negative feelings about the amount or quality of exercise the dog receives, or if the exercise regimen creates problems (for example, the unexercised dog may channel its excess energy into destructive chewing or digging), the owner and/or the dog may need to change.

Is there such a thing as too much exercise for a dog? Not if the dog is in good condition and receives the exercise consistently. Size and breed and even age to some extent are often immaterial. A miniature poodle whose owner leaves it and the baby at the sitter's with five other toddlers and two other dogs can easily cover as many miles and fetch as often as a skilled Laborador retriever does in a weekend of hunting.

How much and what exercise you do with your dog depends entirely on you and your dog. Although you can find references to specific amounts of exercise, some even in terms of breed, age, and sex, these are often merely *body* exercises and often those for dogs whose owners are home all day. If you're told your dog needs at least twenty minutes of walking and fetching exercise daily and you have to drag her down the street and stuff the ball into her mouth to get her to play, is this beneficial, total exercise? If you walk your dog for the prescribed twenty minutes and he's still full of pep, is it beneficial exercise to ignore his needs?

Total Body Exercise

One aspect of weekend dog exercise often overlooked by even the most avid physical fitness fans is the need to exercise the total animal. Many dogs, especially those that prefer the security of a crate, sleep while their owners are absent. When Mukluk and Colonel remain home alone all day, not just their bodies but also their minds and spirits lack stimulation.

Are there such things as mind and spirit exercises? You bet. If Don Boynton opens the back door to let Mukluk charge out and return exhausted two hours later, the dog is certainly getting body exercise. However, if Don accompanies Mukluk, occasionally throwing a ball for him, jogging two miles with frequent changes in pace and direction, issuing simple commands, and pausing to talk to and stroke the Malamute, Don is exercising his dog's body, mind, and spirit. Weekend dog owners who choose to exercise their pets should set total exercise goals.

Strange as it may seem, physical exercise alone can be detrimental. If we take a mouthy, less dominant dog and run her to the point of exhaustion, the dog is happy as long as she drops into sound sleep as soon as she returns home. But what happens if the physically tired dog remains mentally alert, still craving love and attention from her owners? Her physical body is saying, *Lie still, you're too tired to move. Go to sleep.* But her mind is saying, *I'm so tired but I keep thinking about that big dog next door. I wish my owner would come over and pet me now.* At this point many dogs will begin chewing their paws or the rug. If the dog experiences a little bit of a tickle in its ear or on its skin, it will start worrying those areas, too. To be sure, other underlying causes may predispose dogs to skin, ear, or behavioral problems, but dogs that are totally worked out suffer a fraction of the chronic skin, ear, nervous licking, and behavioral problems that afflict their incompletely exercised or unexercised counterparts.

The three components of total body exercise are:

- Physical exercise. This includes activities such as running, jumping, and swimming and should depend on both owner and dog needs.
- Mind exercise. In this category fall games and obedience training, which can be incorporated into the physical exercise.
- Spiritual exercise. These involve giving the dog encouragement during the exercise period, occasionally slowing the pace or even stopping it for a while, just to sit and communicate via voice, touch, and eye contact.

Especially if you're training an exuberant dog, you may find it helpful and more fun to do it while walking or jogging with your pet. For example, instead of teaching Mukluk to come, sit, and stay in their tiny living room, Don Boynton puts on his jogging shorts and trots down the road with the dog at his side. Every so often he stops and puts Mukluk through a particular training sequence. Although outdoor training might involve more distractions, some dogs find the combination of running spurts or brisk walking and short training sessions quite satisfying. Owners that might be bored by both solitary jogging and twenty-minute daily training sessions in the family room may find the combination of training and shared activity much more rewarding. Giving your dog a command, then praising its response, fortifies both mind and spirit. Jogging or walking between commands fortifies the body.

Consistency, Inconsistency, and Conditioning

Before initiating any exercise program for our weekend dogs, we must consider how it relates to our weekend lifestyles. Like all other aspects of weekend dog ownership, inconsistencies can ruin an exercise program. Because few of us can schedule consistent exercise for ourselves, our pets can succumb to our pitfalls. For example, if Steve and Joanie Bennet work as computer programmers all week and do nothing but eat, sleep, and work from Monday through Friday, they can expect sore muscles if they spend Saturday and Sunday splitting and stacking wood or planting the garden. If Colonel spends most of his weekdays sleeping except for an occasional evening romp, he'll also experience some muscle stiffness if he helps Steve and Joanie with their weekend activities. Paper-trained Trinket doesn't even go outside in the winter, so her stiffness always shows up in the spring when Adele begins letting her outside.

Lots of people, even those with Bonded or Dependent views about everything else, think of dogs as wild animals when it comes to exercise. If the Bennets decide to take a two-week hiking vacation, they know they must get in shape for it, but it doesn't cross their minds that sedentary Colonel needs the same conditioning. That weekend dogs need conditioning became painfully clear to me one rainy fall evening several years ago. As I drove down a busy highway, I saw a young man walking along the side of the road wearing a large pack frame full of camping gear. Periodically he stopped, turned around, and squatted down. As I got closer, I realized he was trying to coax a large shepherd mix to keep up with him. The dog looked sore and tired and wet, and seemed to want no part of his master's dream of hiking through scenic New Hampshire. Just before I turned off the highway, I saw the young man pick up the dog and carry it. I doubt that his dream trip, conceived in some downtown Manhattan office, included carrying his sixty-pound dog on top of fifty pounds of gear!

A comical but equally meaningful example popped up in the news a while back. A young couple took their weekend dog, a Saint Bernard, skiing. However, the unconditioned dog became exhausted slogging through the deep snow and had to be rescued by a troop of Boy Scouts. I can hear the incredulous owners saying, "How can this be? Saint Bernards are snow dogs. They're supposed to do the rescuing!" That may be true for an animal trained and worked *daily* to do exactly that, but breed alone does not confer instant physical stamina. Few of us would hesitate to condemn those who attribute certain characteristics to a particular race or group of people, yet we physically stereotype dogs all the time. Before you begin any exercise program with your dog, look at your goal and then evaluate your dog's current life-style and activity. If there's a large gap between what your dog does now and what you eventually want it to do, ease into the exercise program over a period of weeks or even months, depending on the dog's age and condition. As we discussed before, sudden changes unaccompanied by necessary belief changes in both owner and dog seldom become permanent.

Toys for the Weekend Dog

A trip to your local pet shop will reveal as many different dog toys as there are kinds of dogs. In general, pick toys that (a) are sturdy, (b) contain a minimum of dye, and (c) don't look like people-food, or possessions (i.e., lamb chops, shoes, candy bars).

Although sturdy toys are more expensive, nothing's more disconcerting to the weekend dog owner than finding half a toy and a vomiting dog in its crate. Anything that feels soft and flimsy to you will disintegrate when attacked by a pup's razor-sharp teeth or an adult dog's powerful ones, and stuffed animals that have survived three active toddlers will soon be a mere pile of stuffing. All weekend dog owners would prefer not to have to answer certain dreadful questions: Where is the other half of Trinket's little mouse? What happened to the plastic eyes from Colonel's stuffed bear? Has anyone seen the squeaker from Mukluk's elephant?

I recommend undyed or lightly colored toys because dog allergies are becoming more common and the dyes in foods and plastics may be some of the culprits. Although one can easily solve the medical problem by removing the offensive toy, if the dog has become attached to it, you may create an unwanted emotional problem in the process. Although the battle over whether or not dogs perceive color has raged for years, a toy's color matters more to owners anyway.

Because a dog's vision more readily perceives motion than color or detail, dogs may confuse toys that look like shoes and lamb chops with the real thing. To be sure, the dog will follow other cues such as smell, but it's surprising how many weekend dog owners will give the dog an old sweater, shoe, or sock for a toy, then hit the roof when the dog drags around or chews their Sunday best. This can be particularly troublesome if such clothing has been used to play tug-of-war. *Oh boy! A stretchy cashmere sweater hanging on a chair!* The sweater could certainly supply the dog with hours of tugging play, but few weekend owners can afford to indulge such luxuries.

Constructing and Using a Weekend Dog Playground

Do you live in an apartment or condominium with a postage stamp for a backyard? Don't worry. It's not how much space you have; it's how you use that space. Because our schedules can be so hectic, we weekend dog owners can save a lot of time later by spending a little time now constructing a play area for ourselves and our dogs. Not only can the dog enjoy the area while we're gone, we can use it to create total body exercises when we're together.

The size of the play area will depend on how much property you have and how much of it you wish to devote to your dog. If you take delight in your symmetrical flower beds and patio, you may prefer to build your canine playground in some remote corner. If you live in a rustic log cabin in the woods, your dog's playground might include a big chunk of forest. It doesn't really matter as long as you concentrate on total fitness. For example, a good total body exercise involves teaching your dog to walk a narrow beam or plank toward you. One nice arrangement includes a heavy board anchored to cement blocks to ensure stability. If it wobbles unsafely, the dog won't use it. Obviously the size of the board and the number of blocks necessary to support it depend on the size of your dog. However, if you consider such an arrangement unsightly or impractical, a picnic table bench or log will serve just as well for small to medium-sized breeds.

If you anchor your plank securely or use a bench, you can also teach your dog to crawl under it. Often, just lying on the ground and calling the dog will get it to come under the board to you. If not, you can leash the dog, pass the leash under the board, and gently pull the dog toward you, all the while maintaining eye contact and giving cheerful encouragement.

Jumping through hoops, or better, crawling through tubes, also provides good total exercise. For smaller dogs you can use terra-cotta drainage pipes carried by most building suppliers, or you can partially bury old tires in the ground. For all dogs, cardboard boxes opened at both ends are as exciting as they are to kids. Again, you may have to leash the dog and jolly it through the tunnel a few times to get it started, but most dogs catch on quickly.

Many dogs, especially bird dogs or other sight-oriented breeds (greyhounds, whippets, Borzois) love to play catch. Although other breeds may enjoy playing with toys, they may not automatically retrieve them and therefore must be taught. Regardless, catch-and-fetch is one of the most versatile total body exercises because it couples physical activ-

Figure 10–1 Weekend Dog Balance Beams

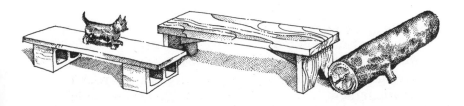

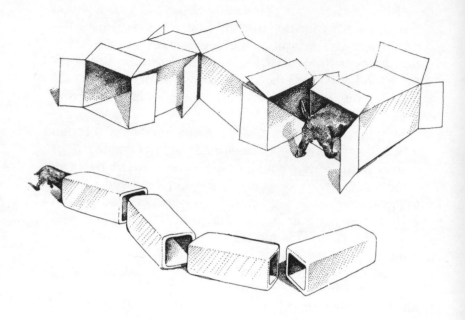

Figure 10–2   Exercise Tubes for the Weekend Dog

ity with a game both pet and owner can enjoy. Once the
dog enjoys playing the game, the ball, Frisbee, or other toy
can become part of its playground. You may simply leave
the toy lying in the play area, or you may suspend it from
a post with a horizontal bar or a tree limb. Don't hang it
from the sort of pole children use in tetherball because
jumping dogs tend to concentrate on the toy and forget
the pole until they hit it. Big dogs enjoy pushing tire
swings around and smaller ones may even learn to jump
through them.

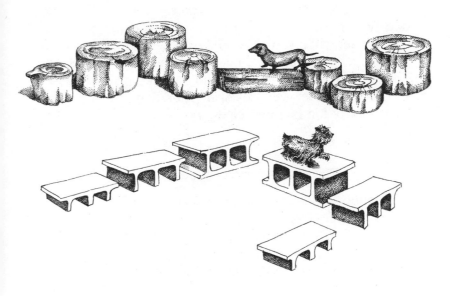

Figure 10–3   Weekend Dog Obstacle Courses

Many dogs also enjoy obstacle courses such as stepping from rock to rock or going up and down stairs. Depending on your feelings about your yard and how much time and effort you want to put into the playground, you can bury rocks, cement blocks, or sections of logs to challenge your dog. Only your creativity limits the combinations. You may also use the stairs in your apartment building or on your patio or back porch. If you're ambitious, you might combine obstacles with a balance beam or tube somewhere in the middle.

Keep in mind that you might have to teach your dog to use the playground and that doing so is part of any total weekend dog exercise plan. However, once you teach the dog how to use the playground, it can enjoy hours of amusement while you're gone. If you keep your dog in an outside kennel, creating a play area within the kennel can do much to relieve tension and boredom. Ideally, you should share the play area with your dog, but dogs can have a lot of fun by themselves, too.

Playmates for the Weekend Dog

Neighborhood kids or your own are great potential playmates for weekend dogs, especially if the children have already discovered or built a playground suitable for a dog, too. Trustworthy preteens and teenagers will often willingly exercise your dog after school for a minimal fee or even for free if you can't do it yourself. Kids who already have to walk the family pet or those who want a pet but for some reason can't have one can make great surrogate companions for your dog when you're busy or gone.

It goes without saying that most dogs enjoy playing with other dogs, too. To ensure companionship and avoid threatening relationships, introduce your dog to other dogs when it's a young pup. If you have neighbors who also have weekend dogs, arrange to let the animals play together. One evening you might have the dogs in your yard and the next evening in your neighbor's playground. Not only will that give your dog more varied exercise and experience, it will give you and your neighbor a breather, too. Although we all love our dogs, sometimes we enjoy them a lot more when we have a few hours apart. In the next chapter we'll discuss the most stable kinds of dog relationships and how to deal with problems should they arise. For now, just keep in mind that two dogs can exercise each other a great deal, and two dogs and two or more people can be a superb exercise combination.

Exercises for the Housebound Dog

Because of her hip problem, Adele Metzger isn't comfortable exercising Trinket outdoors. However, if she's willing, she can do plenty inside. As we mentioned before, catch-and-fetch provides versatile total exercise. Even people confined to wheelchairs can roll or bounce a ball for their dogs. The easiest way to teach a dog to fetch is to begin by slowly rolling the ball or toy by the dog when it's still a young pup. Because of the pup's following reflex, it tends to go after it and pick it up. Lavishly praise the pup and beckon it to you with large sweeping gestures from a crouched position. Older dogs are often reluctant to learn the game, although sometimes imparting an enticing scent to the toy by storing it in the clothes hamper for a few weeks, or (and only as a last resort) rubbing it with a small amount of meat or cheese will spark the interest of a reluctant fetcher.

Naturally, we must tone down indoor games. If the Boyntons play ball with Mukluk in their three-bedroom split level with the same gusto as outdoors, the ninety-pound Malamute could damage a fair number of furnishings. To exercise bigger dogs indoors, invent games of hide-the-toy. Tell your dog to sit while you hide the ball or favorite toy under a chair or couch within the dog's view. When the dog retrieves it, give lavish praise. When the dog gets the hang of the game, you can hide the toy in other rooms and harder-to-find places, such as within a stack of cardboard boxes in a far corner under the bed where Trinket will have to wiggle and worm those extra pounds off to get it. Such a game exercises the mind and spirit more than the body, but even large dogs will be delighted with an indoor version of their favorite game.

Depending on the size of the dog and the size of the house, games involving travel up and down stairs provide good opportunities for total exercise. Be careful not to create such an exuberant game that your dog doesn't pay attention to where it's going. Low-keyed Trinket may perform beautifully chasing and retrieving a ball or toy that Adele throws up the stairs, while big, gallumping Mukluk plays so enthusiastically he could charge up the stairs, miss three or four steps, and fall. With any indoor exercise, we want to relax the dog, not work it into a frenzy that might cause it to injure itself.

Many dogs enjoy hide-and-seek. Children are particularly adept at playing this game with dogs, although adults can also enjoy it. First, have your dog sit and stay while you hide. Once you're hidden, enthusiastically call your pet. Your dog will enjoy it most if you respond with great enthusiasm and affection when it finds you. As with hide-the-toy, you may have to begin by hiding in an obvious place until the dog gets the idea, but most dogs pick it up quickly. Incidentally, playing this game with a young pup will help teach the dog to come.

Except for a very small dog in a very large house, few indoor environments can duplicate the full range of physical activities available to the dog outdoors. However, by increasing the dog's mental and emotional involvement in any game or exercise, you can effectively counter the adverse effects of limited physical activity. Although we ideally want to balance our relationship with the dog so that we fulfill all needs equally, sometimes our erratic schedules make that impossible. However, it is possible to set aside at least some time each day for the dog. I know one weekend dog owner who talks to his dog and plays catch with the dog's favorite toy while he shaves every morning. Another dog accompanies his mistress while she makes the beds and straightens up the bedrooms. When his mistress goes in to shower for work, the dog goes downstairs and helps his master prepare breakfast and feed the baby. These may not sound like much exercise, but they're quite meaningful to a dog. Seize opportunities whenever you can to combine some chore with a little fun exercise for both you and your dog. A runner friend says he could never jog regularly because of boredom, but his new running mate, a German shorthair, changed that.

CHAPTER 11

Sex and
the Weekend Dog

*E*leanor Rossman got Clover and took a part-time job to fill the many empty hours after all her children had grown and left home. After raising three active children, she certainly didn't want to deal with pups, so she had Clover spayed at six months. Now, at age two, Clover's gaining weight rapidly.

"It's because she's spayed," says Eleanor. Sometimes while leafing through the family photo album, she feels guilty about spaying her pet.

"Poor Clover can't ever have babies. Here, have some of Mummy's ice cream."

Five years ago Mary MacComber got her beagle, Ashley, after an intruder tried to break into her home. Although the dog is castrated, he displays dominant behavior around strangers. This posed no problem in the past until Mary and a co-worker at Data International decided to marry. Ashley hates Mary's boyfriend and tries to bite him whenever he spends the night. Mary appreciates all those years of companionship and protection, but it's fast becoming a matter of which she prefers, her dog or her lover.

"Yes sir, that dog's a stud!" George Pickering boasts of his strong male Doberman, Satan. But his pride turns to anger when he has to rush the agonizing dog to the vet's. "Some bastard blasted Satan with cold water while he was breedin' a bitch. He's ruined!" Sure enough, Satan's erect penis will not retract; its own sheath now acts like a tourniquet. The vet's unsure whether he can save the tissue or will have to amputate.

Bill and June Coleson took a lot of time to include their five-year-old son, Bobby, in the training of their Cairn terrier, Scruffy. Now the dog never leaves Bobby's side, practically serving as a nanny as well as a companion. Scruffy responds to Bobby's commands to come, sit, and stay, and the two have formed a strong bond. "It seemed like a lot of work at the time," says Bill of the training required, "but it sure paid off!"

Our own beliefs about sex strongly affect the way we view sex-related behavior in our dogs. In the areas of pet parenthood, neutering, and the human/dog pack structure, Dependent and Independent beliefs often create more problems than they solve. When George Pickering refuses to leash Satan because he insists "a dog's supposed to run free and mate with other dogs," he's setting himself up for as many problems as his neighbor, who believes "that Pickering dog raped my Susie!" If Susie's owner doesn't want her to be bred, he should either spay her or confine her during heat (approximately three weeks twice yearly). Were both of these owners to adopt a Bonded approach, they'd begin to accept full responsibility for their pets. Let's see how our beliefs affect specific sex-related weekend dog problems.

To Breed or Not to Breed

Lack of thought and preparation can turn the miracle of birth into a painful experience for weekend owners who may suddenly find themselves cleaning up after fourteen retriever pups or bottle-feeding four neonatal toy poodles after a long day's work. Weekend dog owners who choose to breed their males may helplessly watch their previously well-behaved dogs mount pillows and people, while still others will collapse in frustration when their females go into heat and their front yards become battlegrounds for fighting males. Unfortunately, as with all such sensitive subjects, ignorance causes problems and guilt monstrously magnifies them.

The weekend dog owner with the temperament and life-style to successfully breed dogs is about as rare as a duck-bill platypus in Manhattan. Sure, you can do it, but it takes an almost superhuman effort within the weekend life-style. Before breeding your dog, ask yourself, "Why do I want to breed my dog?" Do you want to fulfill your own needs? Some owners who plan not to have children themselves act out their own paternal or maternal instincts by breeding their dogs. Regardless of the psychological implications, don't consider breeding until you know what you're getting into. Raising pups not only requires knowledge of your particular breed, its hereditary problems, and how to avoid them, but also a sound background in finance and marketing.

The Mathematics of Reproduction

When George Pickering turns his intact male loose, he's expressing a strong Independent belief. Even those who strongly advocate spaying females will often hedge when it comes to castrating males. The most prolific bitch goes into heat twice a year and produces *at most* fifteen pups per litter. Thus, a bitch can produce a maximum of thirty pups a year.

But how about Satan? On his daily rounds, the Doberman marks an area around George's house approximately one mile in diameter. Within that area live four unspayed females, two that remain confined to outdoor runs accessible to Satan and two that run loose. If these females range from a 20-pound beagle to a 130-pound Saint Bernard, they'll average eight pups per litter. (In general, the smaller the dog, the smaller the litter.) Four females coming into heat twice yearly, capable of producing eight pups per cycle, could therefore produce sixty-four pups. A healthy male like Satan could certainly sire that many pups in a month. Imagine the number of his offspring if he lived in a crowded condominium complex!

"I Can't Neuter My Dog Because . . . "

One reason people often use for not neutering both male and female dogs is that it makes them fat. As we've said before, there's only one thing that makes a dog fat—eating too much. As long as you're in charge of what your dog eats, it need not get fat. Unfortunately, an owner's guilty feelings about neutering a pet, coupled with strong food-equals-love beliefs, almost always generate a fat dog. Because Eleanor Rossman attributes much of her own meaning in life to her role as wife and mother, she feels she's depriving Clover when she has the dog spayed. If Eleanor truly believes that her love for Clover and Clover's love for her have no bearing on the dog's reproductive status, she won't feel guilty.

A common Independent belief holds that neutering isn't natural. That may be true, but then nothing about a weekend dog's life is natural: Is it natural for an intact male to sit alone in his owner's house eight hours a day when dogs a quarter-mile away are barking out the message that a female has gone into heat? Is it natural for Scruffy, when she's in heat twice yearly, to sit locked in the basement for ten days so she doesn't spot the rug with blood? Is it natural for a bitch to be harassed by a pack of fighting males every time she wants to relieve herself in her own backyard? Of course not.

The Bonded view holds that whether we like it or not, our dogs live in an unnatural state as long as they live with people. They're often crowded together in apartments or condominiums where they hear each other continually but may never meet face to face, and will therefore never establish a social relationship with neighborhood dogs, let alone form a pack. And we don't want them to do so because packs can be dangerous. Ask any dog owner who's been besieged by five dogs while walking a poodle, or a mother and weekend gardener who sees a pack bowl over her five-year-old and mow down the marigolds. Packs may be natural in the wild, but there's certainly no place for them in urban or suburban America.

Recognizing that our dogs live an unnatural life, weekend owners should try to relieve the tension our life-style places on them. Because the greatest amount of physical and emotional tension centers around the reproductive organs and their hormones, deciding to spay or castrate one's pet represents a loving and caring choice. Not only does it take a great deal of pressure off the dog, it relieves the owner of the myriad of behavioral and medical problems that often attend an intact animal in our weekend environment. Common conditions such as destructive behavior, urinary marking, and fighting among males decrease. Far better to spay a healthy young female by choice at six months than to cope with sometimes life-threatening surgical removal of an infected uterus from a ten-year-old bitch. Whether or not the weekend dog gets bred, spayed, or castrated is an almost totally emotional issue. And it surely is a personal one.

The Pack vs. the Family

As pack animals, dogs may display dominant or submissive behavior at different times. In the weekend dog household, neither the dog nor the owner is completely in charge.

My experience leads me to conclude that dogs gauge dominance on the basis of sex. Most dominant dogs react more aggressively toward male persons but remain relatively calm around females. Perhaps the animals see the males as equals contending for the dominant position, whereas they view females as nonthreatening. Although I have encountered my share of biters of both sexes, most of these turn out to be submissive animals reacting out of fear. The truly dominant and confident animal doesn't perceive me as a threat. Where my male colleagues may quite literally engage in a war of wills when treating some animals, I may often be able to do it easily, simply because the animal *allows* me to do it.

If Scruffy Coleson lets June clip her nails but runs every time she sees the clippers in Bill's hands, should Bill struggle with the dog to prove he can do the job? Probably not. On the other hand, before the Colesons involved their son in Scruffy's training, the dog refused to allow Bobby Coleson out of the yard or his playmates in. That pack structure had gotten out of hand. Let's go back a few years to when Scruffy first moved in with the Colesons and see how the pack structure evolved. When June and Bill first got Scruffy, she readily came to June but would squat and wet whenever Bill approached her. Although she soon outgrew this habit, she still remained more reserved with Bill.

On the other hand, Scruffy was much more obedient around Bill, especially outdoors.

"I can't understand it," June confided to her neighbor as Scruffy disappeared down the street. "If Bill calls her, she stops dead in her tracks. If I call her, she keeps right on going!"

Scruffy's behavior indicates she recognizes Bill, not June, as dominant in the original pack that included Bill, Scruffy, and June, in decreasing order of power. When the baby arrived, the Coleson pack structure expanded, with Bobby on the bottom rung of the ladder. When Bobby was an infant, the Colesons loved the way Scruffy watched over him, but now it's a pain in the neck. Unless June and Bill want their son's life dominated by the dog, they must teach Scruffy that all people are dominant. To achieve this, everyone must get involved in Scruffy's training. Scruffy must learn to respond to June and Bobby and let them climb above her on the ladder of dominance.

To put the Cairn into a responsive frame of mind, Bill puts Scruffy through her come-sit-stay paces every evening for a few weeks. Then June and Bill begin working the dog together. Bill gives the dog the first command, then June repeats the same command a short time later. Thus we use Bill to set Scruffy up for the correct response to June's command. Then it's Bobby's turn.

When teaching a dog to respond to a child, use the same setup. Once Scruffy consistently responds to June, she and Bobby begin working the dog together. In cases involving very young children and strongly dominant animals, the dog may have to be trained in stages: first to respond to male and female adults, then male and female teenagers, then male and female preteens, and finally male and female toddlers. This may seem like a laborious process, but a dog that learns to respond to simple commands by a three-year-old will never terrorize your children or their playmates.

When the Top Dog's
a Chicken

In our complicated and often threatening society, many people get pets for protection as well as companionship. We've already seen the potentially explosive dilemma the pseudowatchdog creates. But what happens when such an animal is in charge of the weekend household, the leader of the pack? Mike and Jill Iverson married ten years ago and now have two children, an eight-year-old son, Sean, and a five-year-old daughter, Julie. Shortly after they married, Mike bought Siegfried, a male Rhodesian Ridgeback, to protect Jill when he was gone on business trips. Last year the marriage dissolved, leaving Jill with the children and the dog. Since Mike's departure, the dog rarely sleeps through the night, often pacing for hours, emitting low, ominous growls. At first his behavior made Jill feel more secure, but the dog grew so aggressive that one day he bit her hard when she tried to pull him away from the door so a repairman could enter. She shudders to think what would have happened if Sean had been trying to restrain the dog. Siegfried's protective behavior when Mike was away from home has become dangerous.

Is it possible for a previously well-behaved dog to suddenly turn into a tyrant, a sort of canine Jekyll-and-Hyde? To some extent, yes, but it's more a case of the owner having earlier ignored or approved of such behavior. When circumstances change (i.e., when Mike is no longer around to make Siegfried behave), the behavior becomes more apparent.

When beloved family pets suddenly assume the position of head of the household, the people in that household often feel threatened. In general, the pack leader wants to protect the pack, not hurt it, but a dog like Siegfried, with little training or confidence, suddenly thrust into a protective position, can resort to seemingly bizarre behavior.

When Siegfried sees the repairman, all he sees is a threat to himself, Jill, and the children. When Jill tries to hold him back, she interferes with his concentration and his ability to cope with the threat, as well as with his leadership of the pack. Siegfried won't be charitable toward such a challenge and responds by biting his owner. Although we can't classify Siegfried's response as meanness, the fact remains that his distorted view of his role in the Iverson pack is potentially dangerous.

In order to resolve this problem, Jill and the children must redefine Siegfried's role within the family and also help him gain confidence through training. At first, Jill may need Mike's or some other male's help to reestablish her control over the dog. Then she can teach the children to do likewise. The nice thing about using training to reestablish human leadership in the pack is that the dog simultaneously builds self-confidence while the owner regains control.

The Weekend Dog and the Single Owner

Weekend dogs belonging to single owners may create unique problems. Working adults who live alone with their dogs often create life-styles which differ dramatically from those of families, and the weekend dog in a single-person household often assumes a dominant role without the owner realizing such a role reversal has occurred. Let's consider two examples.

Mary MacComber lives a fairly regimented life with her beagle, Ashley. She entertains few guests, and few of her friends have children. Except an occasional dinner date and her annual two-week vacation, her life follows a familiar pattern. Monday through Friday she leaves the house at 7:30 A.M. and returns at 5:00 P.M., at which time she walks the dog. Saturdays, Ashley accompanies her as she shops or runs errands, and they spend quiet Sundays together. If Ashley growls threateningly when young children or adult males approach them on their daily walks, Mary rationalizes the dog's protectiveness. "He's only taking care of me!" As far as Mary's concerned, Ashley behaves perfectly well.

However, Mary began dating a co-worker a year ago. He's a nice man, a divorced father with three young children. Although the romance has flourished between the two people, the relationship between the dog and Mary's lover is terrible. When he brings his children to visit, Ashley sits stiffly at Mary's side, a ridge of erect hairs bristling down his spine. Warning rumbles fill the room whenever one of the children moves. By the time her guests leave, Mary's a wreck. When her friend spends the night, Mary puts Ashley in the basement rather than endure similar antisocial behavior. However, the dog's frenzied barking and scratching at the cellar door create such a ruckus, she invariably feels she must let him out before her neighbors complain.

George Pickering always plays roughly with Satan, chasing the Doberman around the house, getting down on all fours and pretending to fight. "He's my pal," says George. "We have a great time together." If George's girl friend, Leah, stops in to feed the dog when George is out of town, Satan jumps all over her, licks her constantly, and refuses to leave her alone. When George and Leah embrace, the dog tries to squeeze between them.

Although George and Mary have completely different relationships with their dogs, both have unwittingly created situations where the dog views the owner as another dog. In Mary's case, Ashley sees her as a subordinate dog that must be protected, whereas Satan views George as a competitor. In their play sessions, George's larger size confers dominance; however, Satan quickly establishes dominance over Leah when she's alone with him. When George and

Leah are together, Satan is bewildered because he and George are competing for the same property, Leah. Although Satan respects George's dominance sufficiently not to act openly aggressive, he also wants to keep him away from Leah. Because such behavior doesn't have the same antisocial connotations as Ashley MacComber's, many owners might think it funny. However, it usually ceases to be funny when the dog becomes so frustrated and openly aggressive that it harms someone.

In both cases, owners and friends must reestablish control over the dog, creating situations where the dog receives its cues from people rather than vice versa. Like the Colesons, George must begin by training Satan to a complete response to his commands to come, sit, and stay. Then George must work with Leah until Satan recognizes her authority, and Leah must work with others (including young children) until the dog learns to cheerfully respond to all people when given commands. George's protest that "Satan is a one-man dog!" may work fine when it's just the two of them. But when Satan intimidates Leah, the so-called one-man dog is nothing more than an untrained one. And as we discussed in Chapter 7, any beliefs Mary holds that Ashley's behavior proves his desire to protect her are ill-founded. Ashley's behavior, like Satan's, simply says: *Beware, untrained dog.*

Three's Company

Not only do dogs incorporate people into their packs, they incorporate other dogs, too. In Chapter 7 we spoke of the two-dog household and attendant problems. Remember, the difference between a one-dog household and a two-dog one is more than the simple addition of one dog. It's the difference between one dog and a pack. Even if you feel comfortable with your existing pack, you may be able to exercise little control over a bigger one. Weekend dog owners who get a second dog to solve isolation problems must learn ways to make such an addition smoothly.

Increase the Differences, Decrease the Competition

Which pairs do you think will compete more, two male beagle littermates or a four-year-old male Pomeranian and a six-month-old female Saint Bernard? If you answered beagles, you're right. Like people, dogs tend to compete more with and tolerate less those they perceive as equals. In fact, some behaviorists believe that male littermates are the only dog combinations that will fight to the death. In general, when one dog voluntarily goes down or is forced down by the other into the exposed-belly submissive position, the fight stops. If the two dogs are different sizes, breeds, or ages, neither can fully know the other's strengths or weaknesses; consequently, they hold back a bit. Littermates, on the other hand, have studied each other from the beginning and are much less likely to surrender.

In addition to avoiding littermates, weekend dog owners can simplify the integration of a second pet by choosing a dog quite unlike the existing pet. After owning a forty-pound mixed breed, Dufie, for seven years, I had no trouble integrating a half-pound Yorkshire terrier into my household. Even though both males display dominance, they differ so much in size and age that the bigger dog tolerates behavior from the terrier that would cause him to confront a larger dog. At first they seemed to play too roughly with one another, but I soon realized the rough-and-tumble play was simply their way of establishing a pack order. Whenever Dufie felt the Yorkie had overstepped his bounds, he'd flip him over and hold him down with his nose. If the Yorkie bothered him, Dufie curled his lips threateningly and emitted warning growls. In a matter of weeks, the Yorkie knew the rules and no serious confrontations occurred.

If your dog has not shown evidence of aggression and

antagonism toward other dogs and small animals in the past, it probably won't perceive a small, inexperienced pup as a real threat. Don't interfere; adult dogs are extremely tolerant and forgiving of young pups. Let your dogs set their own pack order. If you continually separate two dogs anytime their play seems too rough, the animals will never resolve the pack structure and the tension between them will grow as the younger one becomes more experienced and the older one feels more threatened. Weekend dog owners who run interference for their dogs must recognize that their very life-style prevents full-time monitoring. When the inevitable fight comes, there's a good chance the owner won't be there; and there's an excellent chance the fight will be far more serious than the rough-and-tumble play the owner originally found offensive.

How to Stop a Dogfight

Letting dogs work things out for themselves is easier said than done. If watching your own dogs go at each other is hard, what do you do when a strange dog attacks your dog? It's a tough and emotional situation, even when we logically, intellectually recognize the dogs are only fighting for dominance and won't normally fight to the death. If your beliefs force you to interfere, at least do so in the most beneficial way. Decide which dog is losing and yank its back legs out from under it, causing it to go down—even if it's your own dog. The important thing is to act quickly and surely: the immobilization of the weaker dog depends as much on the element of surprise as on the dog's position. If you act indecisively, giving weak little tugs on the hind legs, you'll only increase the dog's panic and your own chances of being bitten. Before attempting this procedure, make sure you know exactly what you're doing so you can act confidently, swiftly, and safely.

Sound hard? Our society seems to always favor the *underdog,* so pulling the legs out from under a loser may seem like kicking the dog when it's down. But keep in mind that dogs fight primarily for dominance. If one dog recognizes the other's authority, the fight stops. If you attempt to pull off the stronger dog, you'll not only get bitten yourself, you'll enable the weaker dog to recover and *prolong* the fight.

CHAPTER 12

When the Weekend Dog Gets Sick

On his way home from work, George Pickering stops at the vet's to check on Satan.

"He's a lucky dog," says Dr. Dinslow. "He can go home tomorrow, but you'll have to medicate him three times daily for a week and keep him confined until the medication's gone."

As George walks back to his car, he wonders how he can possibly medicate the dog three times a day when he leaves at six A.M. and sometimes doesn't get home until eight P.M. Two nights this week he might not be able to make it home at all.

Eleanor and Bruce Rossman are just about to leave for dinner with friends when Clover begins retching and gagging.

"Wait, we can't go! There's something horribly wrong."

"Come on, Eleanor. You know what a faker she is!"
"No, this is serious. She looks so pitiful."
"Eleanor! She does this every time we go out!"

Siegfried, the Iversons' Rhodesian Ridgeback, has been vomiting after almost every meal for over a week. He's active and responsive, but he's also beginning to lose weight.

"Don't you think we ought to take him to the vet's, Mom?" asks Sean.

"No, dear, as long as he's eating and drinking, I'm sure he's fine. Dogs can take care of themselves. Come on, it's time to go to Grandmother's."

Beliefs and
the Sick Weekend Dog

When weekend dogs get sick, owners once again confront the relationships between their beliefs, their lifestyles, and their pets. Even owners who can retain their Independent or Dependent beliefs when their pets are healthy will flounder when their pets become hurt or ill.

When divorcée Jill Iverson must contend with a sick dog in addition to dealing with kids, car pools, and a full-time job, a delicately balanced life style becomes unhinged. Faced with such a situation, the hurried owner often yields to the illusion that dogs can take care of themselves. Can they? Do domestic dogs possess all the instincts of their wild cousins or all the human instincts necessary to survive urban life? Hardly. In my area, dogs that run loose invariably run into porcupines. Unfamiliar with the species, they usually get too close or even attack, resulting in a snoutful of quills that usually require general anesthesia to remove. Obviously such dogs have lost their natural instincts not to mess with porcupines. On the other hand, I see plenty of dogs that have been hit by cars; dogs don't seem to have any natural instincts to warn them away from moving vehicles. These two situations illustrate that: (a) dogs lack the instincts to deal with certain natural phenomena their wild cousins deal with every day; and (b) they lack the instincts to deal with urban phenomena such as cars, snowmobiles, and garbage trucks which their owners deal with every day.

Weekend dog owners must be aware which instincts their pets do possess. If Dependent believer Eleanor Rossman attributes her own perceptions to her pet, she will likely overrate her dog's ability to deal with traffic. When Jill Iverson turns Siegfried loose to romp in the woods while she and her children organize their weekend campsite, Jill's Independent views lead her to think city-raised Siegfried will automatically be able to take care of himself. Both women may soon find themselves with sick or injured animals. Canine medical problems derive from people problems as often as from dog problems.

Staying Home to Pamper Clover

Dependent owners find it particularly hard to deal with illness. Not only do they project their own feelings onto their pets, making such subjective statements as "It really hurts him," "She's dizzy," or "Her tummy aches," but they also expect their dogs to respond to illness or injury as they themselves do. For example, when Clover vomits once and Eleanor Rossman coos, "Mommy's little girl has a bad tummyache," she voices her belief that Clover vomits for the same reasons and with the same discomfort as she. If Eleanor cancels her dinner engagement because "*I* hate to be alone when I'm sick!" she's attributing her own feelings to the dog. As we learned in the training chapters, dogs will repeat rewarded behavior. Eleanor stops everything to pamper Clover, so Clover repeats the behavior until she automatically vomits every time Eleanor prepares to leave. Other dogs may exhibit nonspecific lameness or whining whenever they're kenneled or left alone. Such illnesses are people problems.

To break such behavior, simply refuse to reward it. Often this is difficult, because even though the dog has frequently faked illness or injury, an owner's guilt and lack of confidence cause hesitation. "I *know* she's a little faker," says Eleanor, "but what if she's *really* sick this time?" The first time Eleanor ignores Clover's vomiting and goes out, she's a nervous wreck until she returns two hours later. The second time, it's a little easier. In a month's time, Clover accepts Eleanor's departures, still with forlorn looks, but the vomiting stops.

Letting Siegfried Fend for Himself

At the other extreme stand owners who believe dogs can diagnose and treat their own illnesses and injuries. For example, Siegfried charges into the woods surrounding the Iversons' campsite, finds a nearby brook, and plunges in, unmindful that a sharp rock has gashed his left rear footpad. After cavorting in the water, he snuffles through the underbrush, uncovers some buried debris left by previous campers, and wolfs down some decomposing leftovers before ambling back to the camp.

When he gallops across the picnic blanket leaving bloody footprints, the children shout for Jill. "Mommy, Siggy's bleeding!" Jill ignores the dog's gleefully wagging tail and orders him away. As he leaves, Siegfried vomits a large foul-smelling mass on the blanket. The next morning Jill checks his foot; all bleeding has stopped and Siegfried seems to be keeping it clean himself.

"Good. Maybe that'll slow you down."

Siegfried doesn't eat that day. The next day he eats a little, but vomits the food immediately. In his excitement over unearthing the garbage, he's inadvertently swallowed a rock, too big to either vomit or pass. However, because

Siegfried is such a big, strong dog and because Jill's first solo camping trip with the children turned out to be more hectic than she expected, she prefers to assume the dog will heal himself. In the case of the cut footpad she's right, although a pressure bandage would have stopped the bleeding sooner. However, the rock must be removed surgically because there's no way Siegfried can treat it himself.

Will the Really Sick Dog Please Lie Down?

How can we distinguish between genuine sickness, temporary discomfort, or outright faking? Learn to recognize the most common danger signals related to common problems:

Symptom	Problem
Prolonged or repeated vomiting or diarrhea	Foreign bodies such as rocks, toys, bones; tumors
Vomiting or diarrhea with blood	Severe viral infections; poisons
Labored breathing	Diaphragmatic hernias (often associated with trauma); congestive heart failure
Distended abdomen (bloat)	Twisted stomach; gas buildup; uterine infections; tumors
White or pale gums	Shock; blood diseases; internal bleeding
Prolonged seizures	Epilepsy; head trauma; poisoning

Symptom	Problem
Blood from any orifice (mouth, rectum, penis, vagina, nose, ears, eyes)	Trauma; blood diseases; tumors
Prolonged bleeding from any wound	Clotting diseases; damage to major vessels

Whenever your dog exhibits any of these signs, call your veterinarian to determine whether the dog should go in for an immediate examination. Here again, heed what's normal for your dog. How will you know if your dog's gums are pale or white if you've never looked in your dog's mouth? Examine your pet today, while it's healthy. If you're still not sure about the pinkness of its gums, press your index finger firmly against the gum above an upper canine tooth (fang). When you release it, you'll see a pale pressure spot on the gum that will disappear as the blood returns to the area. Were your dog in shock, you'd see no such color change.

How will you know if your dog has a fever if you've never determined its normal temperature? In ten years of practice I have seen all degrees of wet, dry, hot, and cold noses, and none that I'd consistently associate with a sick or healthy dog. To take a dog's temperature, use a standard human *rectal* thermometer, available at most drug stores, following the manufacturer's recommendations regarding insertion and when and how to read the device. The procedure is exactly the same in dogs, including the possibility that some additional help may be needed to prevent excessive movement. Usually having someone steady the dog's head and distract it with rapid cheerful talking or singing is sufficient.

Normal dog temperature runs from 101°F. to 102.5°F., so you must determine what is normal for your dog. If Clover's temperature normally runs slightly above 102.5°F., a temperature of 103°F. may signal less of a problem for her than for normally 101°F. Satan. If George Pickering just opens the back door and turns Satan loose twice a day, how will he know if Satan suffers bloody diarrhea? How will Eleanor recognize Clover's significant vomiting if she gives her table scraps and other foods that could easily upset the dog's stomach? As with so many weekend dog problems, you can more easily determine weekend dog illnesses by controlling the variables. If we don't define normal, if we don't control our dogs' comings and goings, if we view our dogs as little people or wild animals, we waste valuable time sorting through uncontrolled variables when our dogs become sick or injured.

The Weekend Dog First-Aid Kit

Every weekend dog owner should assemble a simple first-aid kit. This inexpensive collection may be kept in a small box where you can easily get to it, and it should contain:

> Kaopectate or Pepto-Bismol
> Hydrogen peroxide
> Rectal thermometer
> Clean washcloths or gauze sponges
> Elastic bandages
> Roll of one-inch adhesive tape
> Buffered aspirin

In addition, tape a card with the following information to the lid of the box:

> Veterinarian's name, address, and phone number
> Dog's weight
> Dog's birth date
> Normal temperature
> Normal diet and feeding schedule

Vaccination history
Any pertinent medical history (including medications the dog is taking)

Often the vet will ask the dog's weight, age, and normal condition to help diagnose the problem and/or prescribe home treatment. Although you may think you know this information like the back of your hand, it can totally slip your mind in an emergency. Periodically update the card to reflect changes in weight, diet, or medical status.

Simple First Aid for the Injured Weekend Dog

If you think your dog has been injured but you're not sure, always call your veterinarian. Practically all vets offer some kind of off-hour emergency service and many metropolitan communities even have full-time emergency clinics. However, don't just grab the phone the instant your dog falls or gets hit by a car. Take a few minutes to evaluate the situation. Can you detect any of the major danger signals? Review the list on pages 166–67 if necessary. If you have trouble remembering it, make a copy and keep it in your first-aid kit. The more information you can give the vet, the more he or she can help you and your dog.

When you encounter trauma or injury:

• *Keep calm.*
• If necessary, carefully move the animal to a safe place, using a blanket or board if one is handy. It's surprising how many people leave a dog on the road because they're afraid to move it. Not only does the injured animal become a hazard for other vehicles, it often gets hit again. If you're concerned the dog may bite you, fashion an effective makeshift muzzle from a nylon stocking or piece of gauze. Make a half hitch over the top of the muzzle, bring the ends around the muzzle,

Figure 12–1 How to Muzzle Your Weekend Dog

and make another half hitch under the chin; then bring the ends of the stocking or gauze behind the ears and tie them in a bow.

• If you spot hemorrhage, apply pressure to the area(s) if possible, using gauze squares or washcloths, holding them in place with elastic bandages.

• Quickly review the danger signs and note which ones, if any, are present.

• Call the veterinarian and clearly describe the details and symptoms. Have the dog beside you if possible so you can provide any additional information the vet may request.

Lameness

Whenever the dog exhibits lameness, first determine whether or not the animal has broken any bones. One helpful diagnostic trick is to hold up the opposite leg; if the lameness affects the right front leg, hold up the left front one. If the dog has broken its right front leg, it will throw its weight onto you rather than on the damaged leg. If the dog puts the leg down, chances are the problem's in the soft tissue (muscles, tendons, ligaments) or joints. In that case, treating with rest and aspirin sometimes works well. You can give a twenty-pound dog up to one aspirin three times daily with no bad side effects. Large, seventy- to eighty-pound dogs can generally handle up to two aspirins three times daily.

Aspirin can also be quite effective in relieving the stiffness of arthritis that afflicts older animals. Owners whose older weekend dogs are relatively inactive on weekdays but run around more on weekends may only need aspirin for Monday-morning stiffness. You can also safely administer aspirin throughout the weekend to prevent the stiffness. Because aspirin can cause upset stomachs in some dogs, just as it does in some people, I prefer a buffered aspirin given with food. If the lameness appears suddenly and the animal does not respond to aspirin, or if it responds but the lameness returns as soon as you discontinue the aspirin, the animal should be examined by your vet.

Lacerations

Cuts, especially on footpads, are a common weekend dog injury because dogs that are confined all week may be less agile than their free-roaming counterparts. Also, weekend dog owners are more likely to head for unfamiliar terrain with their pets on weekends. The combination of poor conditioning, unfamiliar terrain, and the joyful exuberance that often accompanies such outings often results in strains, cuts, and bruises. While aspirin will often control any discomfort, it does nothing for bleeding, and depending on the location of the laceration, bleeding can be a minor or extremely serious problem.

If the cut is in the footpad, the bleeding can be profuse because the pad works like a sponge. Although there are no major blood vessels in the pads, there are numerous little ones which may continually ooze, particularly if the dog licks the foot or walks on it. Pressure bandages usually control such hemorrhaging. Use clean washcloths or gauze

pads, secured with elastic wraps. When bandaging the foot
or lower leg, be sure to include the entire foot; otherwise
the bandage may act like a tourniquet when you apply
enough pressure to stop hemorrhage, thereby damaging
healthy tissue. Sometimes it's necessary to cover the last
inch or so of the elastic wrap with adhesive tape and then
continue the adhesive onto the dog's hair to keep the
bandage from slipping.

Similar bandages may be used on cuts farther up the
leg. Such cuts may present much more serious problems
because a dog's leg between the thigh and foot contains
mostly skin, bone, major blood vessels, tendons, ligaments,
nerves, and very little soft muscle or fat tissue to absorb
damage. A lacerated blood vessel immediately above the
foot is as serious as slashed wrists in a human. Unless shal-
low or superficial, these cuts should be examined by your
veterinarian.

Keep in mind that pressure bandages are merely to control hemorrhage and do not necessarily promote healing.
Remove the bandage after twenty-four hours; if there's still
bleeding, the wound may need to be stitched. Blood-
soaked bandages create a moist, dark, and warm environment around the wound—everything infectious bacteria
need to grow—so don't leave one on more than a day or
two. If you think the bandage should be on longer,
chances are the dog will need antibiotics to control infection, even if stitching is not necessary. Let your veterinarian make this decision.

How you remove a bandage depends on you and your
dog. Although there are preparations available to supposedly dissolve the adhesive, it's been my experience that
they are no faster than doing it manually. Furthermore,
these products often have strong odors which animals find
more bothersome than the manipulation. There are two
ways to remove a bandage manually: you can gradually
work the tape loose from the hair or quickly pull it off. If
you apply your bandage correctly, only an area the diam-

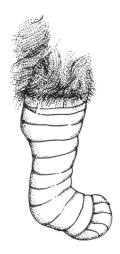

Figure 12–2 Notice that when the foot is correctly band-
aged, the toes are completely covered.

eter of the dog's leg and one-half to two inches wide (the
bigger the dog, the wider the area) is actually taped to its
hair. Once this is removed, the rest of the bandage can be
easily unwound. I find it helps a lot to have one person
remove the bandage while another holds the dog's head,
establishes eye contact, and keeps up a steady stream of
cheerful conversation for distraction.

When you encounter any kind of laceration, concentrate
on controlling hemorrhage. Don't waste valuable time
trying to wash or medicate a freely bleeding wound. If
there's no hemorrhage, use hydrogen peroxide to clean
the area. However, if the dog is licking the wound and
bandaging isn't necessary, don't use anything on it, because peroxide will often cause the dog to vomit. Consult
your veterinarian to determine whether any additional
treatment or examination is necessary.

First Aid for the Sick Weekend Dog

If you think your dog may be ill, but you're not sure, you may want to try a few simple home treatments for more common problems.

Anorexia: Loss of Appetite

If the dog ignores food but acts fine otherwise, chances are it just isn't hungry. Remember, it's normal for a dog not to eat once in a while. However, if you're concerned, offer a *tiny* bit of something bland but palatable like chicken or low-fat cottage cheese. If the dog wolfs this down but refuses its regular dog food, it's probably just resting its digestive system. If the loss of appetite persists for more than forty-eight hours, have the dog examined. Using table food violates my earlier recommendations, but if you're on your way out of town for an all-day conference and need a little reassurance that the dog will be all right until you get home, this simple test may be worth any temporary unwanted associations the dog might make.

Vomiting and Diarrhea

If the dog vomits or has diarrhea once or twice but seems normal otherwise, give *nothing* by mouth for at least eight to ten hours. Remember, dogs are gulpers rather than chewers so they've retained the ability to vomit easily as a protective mechanism. *Oh, oh,* says Satan's digestive track, *I shouldn't have eaten that garbage*—and up it comes. Quite often after vomiting or diarrhea have cleared irritants from the system, it remains hypermotile (moving too fast) and needs time to regain its natural rhythm and heal itself. If you equate eating and drinking with good health in your dog, resist urging it to immediately eat and drink, even if it wants to. Remember the gastrocolic reflex? As soon as anything goes into the system, the entire system is stimulated, producing highly acidic digestive enzymes in response to either food or water;

these hit the irritated lining of the stomach or intestinal track and the system responds by getting rid of them (continued vomiting and diarrhea). In order to avoid this problem, you must break the cycle by putting nothing into the system for at least eight to ten hours. However, you may administer a protectorant such as Kaopectate or Pepto-Bismol to gently coat the irritated lining during this interval. Give this at the rate of one tablespoon per twenty pounds of body weight every six hours.

To give the medication, tilt the dog's head back and tip it slightly to one side. Holding the mouth *gently* closed, pull the skin around the mouth outward on the upper side of the muzzle, exposing the teeth and forming a pocket. Use a turkey baster or syringe to slowly introduce the liquid into this pocket. By holding the mouth gently, you prevent the dog from shaking its head and spraying medication over everything. This position also enables the dog to swallow easily when it feels the medication flowing into its mouth. A spoon may also be used, but it's often much more awkward to handle. Do this outdoors if possible and have a damp washcloth and old towel handy for cleanup. If after twenty-four hours the animal is still vomiting or if diarrhea persists, take the dog to your veterinarian.

Once the digestive system quiets down, begin offering small amounts of water over a twenty-four-hour period. Put an ice cube in a bowl; as it melts, the dog laps the water. When the ice cube is gone, give the dog another one.

If after a day on just water you detect no vomiting or diarrhea, begin the dog on the bland diet described in Chapter 9. As the dog improves, gradually switch it over to its regular diet and feeding schedule. The important thing is not to rush things. A dog can survive without food or water for twenty-four hours, on just water for another twenty-four, and on small amounts of food and water for another twenty-four. Keep in mind that digestive enzymes flow in proportion to the amount of food or water put into the system. If the dog eats or drinks a lot, a lot of digestive juices will flow. In an irritated system these enzymes will cause more irritation, stimulating continued vomiting and/ or diarrhea. As long as the dog acts okay and the vomiting and/or diarrhea ceases, don't rush it. Again, if you have any doubt, call your veterinarian.

Schedule of Treatment for
Simple Vomiting or Diarrhea

Day one:	Withhold all food and water. Give Kaopectate or Pepto-Bismol every six hours.
Day two:	Offer small amounts of water or ice cubes. Continue Kaopectate or Pepto-Bismol.
Day three:	Begin small feedings of bland diet. Feed half the *normal* amount usually fed. Divide the bland diet into three to six small feedings. Continue with ice or small amounts of water. Continue with Kaopectate or Pepto-Bismol.
Day four:	Replace one-quarter of the bland diet with the dog's regular dog food. Continue feeding half the usual amount of food, divided into three to six small feedings.
Day five:	Feed half bland diet and half regular dog food. Increase total amount fed to three-quarters of dog's usual food intake.
Day six:	Feed one-quarter bland diet, three-quarters regular diet. Feed normal amount of food.
Day seven:	Feed regular diet in regular amount.

The number of feedings should be decreased at the rate of one per day beginning on day five until the dog reaches its normal feeding schedule. If the dog does not continue to improve, have it examined. Obviously the four-times-daily medication and multiple feedings may pose problems for working owners. However, if multiple feedings are not possible, it is far better to leave *less* food and water than whole bowlfuls.

Poisoning

Strict regulations governing the manufacture and sale of insecticides, fertilizers, rodent killers, and other dangerous substances have reduced the incidence of deliberate or accidental dog poisoning. However, accidental poisonings from antifreeze, medications, and plants (including marijuana) still occur. If you suspect your dog has ingested a harmful substance, quickly evaluate its condition and obtain as much information about the substance as possible:

- What is the name of the substance? Get the brand and chemical components if possible.
- How much did the dog ingest?
- How long ago did this happen?

Armed with this information, and the dog beside you if possible, call the vet. If the substance should be removed from the dog's stomach, your vet may recommend that you give it hydrogen peroxide to induce vomiting, followed by Kaopectate or Pepto-Bismol to soothe any irritation. Having these products readily available in your first-aid kit can save a half-hour's drive to the vet's or a frustrating search for an all-night pharmacy.

Never give anything to induce vomiting until you consult your veterinarian. Many substances such as medications and plants should be vomited, but acids, furniture polishes, ammonia, and other corrosive substances should *not,* because vomiting such irritants causes *more* damage to the mouth and esophagus (tube connecting the mouth to the stomach). You supply the information; let your vet supply the treatment.

Finding the Perfect Vet

What do you look for when you need a physician? Someone nearby? Someone you can talk to, who makes you feel comfortable confiding even your most intimate problems? Well, you should look for those same traits in your vet. Here's a set of questions that will help you select the ideal vet for your weekend dog:

- Do you feel comfortable talking to this person? Does he or she intimidate you in any way?
- Are you comfortable with the way the vet handles and relates to your dog?
- Is the vet open to suggestions, including requests for a second opinion or referral to another practitioner? Does he or she openly criticize other vets or clients?
- Is some form of emergency or off-hour coverage provided?
- Is the vet willing to speak to you on the phone and recommend home remedies if appropriate, or does he or she always insist on seeing the animal?
- Are the rates reasonable and within your budget? It costs money to maintain well-equipped facilities and they obviously can provide more services for your pet; however, many excellent practitioners operate on a shoestring. Far better to see one of these regularly to *maintain* your dog's good health than postpone medical care because of the cost until some crisis occurs.
- Is he or she the kind of person you'd want to have as a friend?
- Is the facility clean?
- Does the facility have hours that fit into your schedule? Can you make special arrangements to drop your pet off on your way to work or during your lunch hour if you have scheduling problems?
- Is the vet willing to explain what he or she has done or plans to do to your pet and why?

The weekend dog owner's willingness to be open and honest can change Dr. Don't-Bother-Me into Dr. Right. If Dr. Dinslow prescribes four-times-daily medication for Satan, he undoubtedly wants the dog to get better and recommends the treatment he feels best suits the dog. However, other treatments may better match George Pickering's weekend life-style. In some cases, the veterinarian may suggest a dog remain hospitalized a few days longer until its owner can be home to spend more time with it or it can take care of itself. Or the vet may switch to one of the newer, albeit often more expensive, antibiotics one can administer less frequently.

Nothing more fully disrupts owner, dog, and veterinarian communication than an owner's blanket acceptance of an incompatible treatment regime. If the dog doesn't respond because the owner won't or can't carry out the treatment, another load of guilt comes aboard. Sometimes owners feel so bad about their failure to follow the vet's orders, they simply take the dog to another vet for the same prescription, just to avoid the former vet's criticism. If your vet tells you to medicate your Great Dane four times a day and bathe it twice weekly, but you work full-time and live in a studio apartment with only a shower, *say so*. Veterinarians aren't miracle workers; they can only do as much as you're willing to let *and help* them do. What may seem like an insurmountable scheduling or medicating program usually has an alternate approach. If you're honest about your own needs and limitations, your veterinarian can consider other options and together you can work out one that maintains your pet's good health within your weekend life-style.

Weekend dog owners need good rapport with their vets for another, very important reason. If your dog is sick and vomiting occasionally or having bouts of diarrhea and you can't leave work to nurse it, what do you do? You either hospitalize the dog or contend with the mess when you get home from work. Hospitalization, in theory, should be only for those animals too sick to be properly treated at home. And there are vets who refuse to hospitalize an animal for the owner's convenience if they believe that medically the dog's condition doesn't warrant it. Some of these practitioners even argue that a mildly sick animal is likely to pick up more infection in a hospital than at home. Perhaps that's true if the dog is in a household with someone home all day to provide care. However, for the working owner whose choice is often to crate the dog, knowing it will lie in its own wastes, or face the destruction of furnishings, it's worth the risk. Veterinarians who are sensitive to the special needs and dilemmas of weekend dog owners often will let the owner drop off the dog on the way to work and pick it up on the way home. To be sure, you have to pay for this service, but you're also getting peace of mind for the price.

CHAPTER 13

Old Age, Death, and Euthanasia

"***H***ey Doc!" John Brown hails me in the crowded shopping center parking lot. "I want you to put that pup of mine to sleep."

"How come?"

"He's getting too big. Eats too much."

During the six months that Clover's health fails with degenerative kidney disease, Eleanor Rossman takes the dog to seven different vets, always refusing to leave her for any diagnostic work-up because "Clover and I both hate hospitals." In her travels, Eleanor has amassed eight different kinds of medication which she administers on an irregular basis, depending on *her* feelings about the dog's condition. When the dog becomes so ill she refuses food and water and won't even get up to relieve herself, Eleanor is forced to hospitalize her.

Dave Grummond works a swing shift. His fourteen-year-old English setter, Daisy, has been at the vet's for two weeks with nonresponsive heart failure. Although it's difficult for him to do it, Dave has the dog put to sleep.

"We've had a real good life together and I want the best for both of us."

That evening, Dave takes a long walk with his new pup, Marigold. Although he's only had her for two months, a strong bond is already forming between him and the Airedale. He's especially glad to have her at his side now.

Taking Our Beliefs to the End

Although most people recognize old age and death as natural parts of life, they still agonize over these inevitabilities when they involve loved ones, human or canine. Do those who view dogs as displaced wild animals face old age and death more gracefully? Sometimes. However, a lot of people manage to maintain Independent beliefs right up to the end, before massive guilt strikes. Why?

Those who insist that dogs are a totally independent species should view old age, death, and euthanasia *whenever and under whatever circumstances* as quite natural. However, few of the Independent crowd can rationalize the naturalness of a murderous '79 Chevy or their own neglect of serious medical problems they thought their dogs could handle. Nor are there many John Browns around who can casually euthanize a pup merely because it's growing too big. Viewing some aspects of old age like arthritis and impaired vision or hearing (which greatly increase any dog's chances of being hurt if left to fend for itself) as self-healing, strains even the strongest Independent beliefs. What can these people say when their wild-dog beliefs cause their dogs increased stool production, diarrhea, constipation, weight loss, or other physical problems? Doubts begin to erode former confidence: "Should I start administering aspirin? Should I switch diets?" Having believed for so long that dogs can take care of themselves, they now dread making any changes or starting anything that could complicate already overly complicated lives.

Dependent believers in many ways suffer even more when confronting the old age and death of their pets because they invariably see these conditions as they affect themselves and other people. Consequently they may feel obligated to request extensive, and expensive, medical treatment for their dogs because "that's what they do for people." Similarly, because euthanasia is a taboo human consideration, Dependent adherents cut themselves off from this means of resolving some of our most distressing problems with our dogs.

The Bonded approach, as always, recognizes that owner and dog work together for the mutual benefit of both. Dave Grummond knows his conscientious care has added years to Daisy's life-span compared to that of her wild cousins. However, he also realizes that there may come a time when the quality of Daisy's life and the changes it necessitates in his own are no longer acceptable, and he may have to consider euthanasia. To him, death and/or euthanasia are not failure or cop-out positions; they are always available choices, and often the responsibility of a caring owner.

Regardless of an owner's prior beliefs about dogs, when this stage of ownership arrives, personal beliefs about old age and death dominate; doubts and fears about old age and death for ourselves always color how we handle these phenomena when they involve our pets. I've seen previously calm and mellow individuals act quite belligerent and resentful at the first sign of aging or infirmity in their animals, while formerly oblivious and neglectful ones suddenly grow overprotective at the first sign of gray hair. The former owner may request euthanasia when he or she first spots joint stiffness, whereas the latter may demand sophisticated life-support systems and rare diagnostic paraphernalia when it becomes clear that advanced age has arrived. Carefully evaluate your beliefs about human old age and death so you won't suffer unduly when the vet—or the driver of the car that hit your dog—frowns and says, "I'm sorry but ..." Here are some questions that will help you objectively evaluate such beliefs:

- Does it make you sad when you think of your dog growing old?
- Do you recognize special (and good) things your older dog does that it didn't do when it was a pup (stays closer to home, barks less, behaves better)?
- Do you view inevitable death of your pet in terms of "I'll never get another dog! I can't bear to go through this again"?
- Does death frighten you?
- Do you wish you and your family could live forever?
- Do you view old age and death as parts of the natural progression of all living things?
- Are you more concerned about the quality of your pet's life than the actual span of time that life encompasses?

The Twilight Years

Let's look at a typical weekend household confronting and resolving some of the common problems associated with old age in dogs. When Dave Grummond hospitalizes old Daisy and faces the possibility that she may die or he may have to have her put to sleep, he recalls the other times he altered his life for her. Over the past two years he's treated her arthritic hips and shoulders with aspirin. When she began gaining weight, he switched from free-choice dry food to a special canned food that he doled out in small amounts whenever his schedule permitted, and when her eyesight failed, he sprayed a lightly scented cologne eighteen inches from the top and bottom of the stairs and at the doorways to help her find her way. When he walked her, he guided her with a bright flashlight, and when she ventured out alone, he flashed the back porch light to call her, after her hearing failed.

Because these considerations for her physical deterioration seemed to make her more comfortable, Dave didn't mind the inconvenience; but he found himself unprepared for the behavioral changes that attended Daisy's aging. Like many elderly dogs, Daisy's diminished senses of hearing, sight, and smell made her feel vulnerable in strange surroundings. She became so disoriented and confused, Dave had to begin walking her on a leash. Because her hips hurt, Daisy feared any motion toward her rear end, especially by children, whose faster motion and higher-pitched voices threatened her. Once she even snapped at Dave's grandson. Shortly thereafter, Dave convened the grandchildren to explain about Daisy's infirmities and to warn against rough-and-tumble play. Although the children responded beautifully by treating Daisy with the respect they felt an old dog deserved, Dave still worried that some newcomer, especially a child, would rush at the unsuspecting dog and get bitten. Before long, Daisy never ventured outdoors without adult supervision.

Common Signs of Old Age in Dogs

Decreased eyesight
Decreased hearing
Rear-end stiffness; reluctance to move
Increased protectiveness and aggressive behavior
Loss of stamina
Loss of ability to digest certain foods or types of foods

"Do Everything You Can, Doc"

When Eleanor Rossman faces the impending death of her cocker spaniel, Clover, she understandably cries, "Do everything you can!" However, like many people, Eleanor doesn't realize the full implications of such a request. Depending on your veterinarian's facilities, doing *everything* may range from providing limited supportive care and making the animal comfortable to placing the dog in a special intensive-care unit, complete with oxygen and intravenous therapy, electrocardiograms, electroencephalograms, blood tests, X rays, and round-the-clock nursing. The difference can amount to hundreds of dollars a day.

Owners who feel responsible for some trauma such as a car accident or illness ("I should have been driving more carefully"; "I never should have let her run loose while I was at work"; "I should have treated the vomiting sooner") will probably feel too guilty to raise the issue of money. Even though money may play a critical role in how far they wish to go with treatment, most owners often feel disloyal discussing it. How much should one spend to save a loved one? Furthermore, in my experience, working people or those who spend a lot of time away from home are more prepared for their pets to suddenly die or become magically healthy than they are for an intermediate invalid condition that will greatly disrupt their lives. Before you commit yourself, your pet, and your vet to treatment, determine the following:

- What is the prognosis? If the pet survives, will it be normal? Will it require special care? Can you offer that care within your current life-style? Are you willing to change your life-style to accommodate the dog?
- What are the immediate and long-term financial implications of the dog's problem? Most veterinarians will willingly give estimates.

• What are your choices? Not surprisingly, the choices remain the same: (a) accept the situation as it exists (do nothing); (b) change the situation (treat the dog); (c) get rid of the dog (euthanasia).

I equate getting rid of the dog and euthanasia because one should never take an unhealthy animal to a humane society or foist it off on some unsuspecting person simply because one lacks the courage to make a decision about death.

Death and Euthanasia

Death and euthanasia pose similar problems. Although some may argue that euthanasia is unnatural, we already recognize that much of our weekend relationship with our dogs is naturally unnatural. Let's examine the two major types of illness and injury that most often end in death or euthanasia.

Death Preceded by Traumatic Illness or Injury

We'll use the term traumatic death to describe that preceded by sudden severe (or acute) illness or injury. It is traumatic not only in the sense that the animal experiences massive physical damage in a short period of time, but also in terms of its devastating effect on the owner. When a pet dies suddenly, either by accident or severe illness, owners often feel cheated, betrayed, or angry, but these emotions invariably turn into guilt:

"If only I had been home."
"He's never crossed that road before."
"Did she suffer?"
"Why didn't I keep her chained up?"

Because many veterinarians often *do* hold the owner responsible for whatever happens to the pet, doctors and guilt-ridden owners can easily fall into an adversary relationship. The vet assumes the role of protector and savior of poor defenseless animals, while the guilty owners view themselves as irresponsible persons who should never own a dog. Even if the vet doesn't feel this way, an owner of a traumatized pet usually thinks he or she does anyway.

How can you avoid this situation? The key is confidence. If we feel comfortable with our weekend dog relationship, there's no need for us to feel guilty about accidents and diseases that befall our pets. This in no way means we won't openly grieve if something does happen, but if we have confidence that we've designed the best life for ourselves and our dogs, we'll focus on our *loss,* not our guilt.

The death of a puppy deserves special mention because it is often the most traumatic, especially for the individual who had doubts about his or her fitness as a dog owner. Those who didn't have time to get their pups vaccinated because they were in the process of changing jobs may find themselves awash with guilt when the pup succumbs to distemper or Parvo virus infections. Owners who just never got around to building a sturdy pen or secure run are crushed by remorse when the pup is hit by a car or gets into the neighbor's paint thinner. Owners who find notes from their landlords giving them twenty-four hours to get rid of the dog or move may have to confront the possible euthanasia of a perfectly healthy animal.

To be sure, all of these situations can be avoided with careful planning and preparation *before* you get your pup. But if it happens—by disease, accident, or euthanasia—experience grief, not guilt, and learn from the experience.

Facing Death with the Chronically Ill and Geriatric Dog

Chronic illnesses are those that seem to creep up on the dog and just go on and on. Unlike accidents or severe viruses like Parvo that may kill a healthy pup in a matter of days, chronic diseases of the heart, kidney, or liver produce a long-term seesaw pattern of good and bad days for dog and owner alike. Although chronic illnesses rarely have the dramatic effect of acute or traumatic ones, they can be just as devastating. When the Grummonds or the Rossmans watch a beloved family pet slowly deteriorate, the specter of death or euthanasia haunts their daily lives. Six months ago, Dave Grummond made an appointment with Daisy's vet to discuss both medical and behavioral signals he should look for and to learn the mechanics of treatment, death, and euthanasia. He was so distraught about the meeting, he made a list of questions so he wouldn't forget anything. His list provides a model for any owner facing the impending death of a pet.

- How much time can we add to Daisy's life by extensive treatment if it becomes necessary? Will the quality of that life be good?
- If Daisy dies at home, what should I do?
- How does a vet put a dog to sleep? What happens to the remains?
- May I bury her at home?
- Can she be cremated? Can I keep the ashes?

The vet answers each question thoroughly:

"First of all, at fourteen, Daisy has enjoyed the normal life-span for her breed. You can expect the sorts of problems she has now to continue and gradually worsen. If a crisis occurs, especially if it involves her heart, we can maintain her with oxygen and intravenous therapy, medication, and cage rest, but her symptoms may recur as soon as we remove this support. Also, if Daisy has a crisis shortly after you and your wife leave for work, she may suffer hours of pain before you return.

"I use a strong intravenous drug for euthanasia. The animal goes down the same way it does for anesthesia, only respiration and heartbeat cease. It usually takes less than a minute. Like most vets, I prefer that you sign a release. You may choose to be with Daisy during euthanasia if you wish.

"Whether Daisy dies at home or here, this town permits home burial of pet animals. If you want to bury her somewhere else, though, make sure you check local regulations. In more populated areas, laws forbid such burial. She can also be cremated, and you may keep the ashes."

Dave feels much better when he and Daisy leave the vet's office. Now at least he has some idea what to expect when the time comes.

Compare Dave's approach to Eleanor Rossman's. When Clover begins to fail, Eleanor rushes from vet to vet, demanding the newest drugs. In addition, she reads medical columns in popular magazines and discusses Clover's ailments with her bridge club. Anything anyone suggests, Eleanor tries: vitamins, minerals, laxatives, special diets, most of them recommended for human problems Eleanor believes parallel Clover's. If a vet tells her Clover's problems are age-related and recommends measures to make the dog comfortable rather than promising to cure her, Eleanor looks for another vet. Meanwhile, she plies Clover with all kinds of people foods and medications, dismissing the vet's recommended diet as "too bland and unappetizing for my little girl." Thus, while Dave spends his time preparing for the end, Eleanor spends her time denying it.

Although no one enjoys watching a chronically ill or geriatric animal slowly decline, one does have a chance to prepare, to ease the transition to the inevitable.

Love Can Mean Letting Go

A wise friend once said to me, "The ultimate act of love is knowing when to let go." Nowhere else is this more true than when it comes to euthanasia. Unfortunately, many dog owners consider euthanasia a sign of their own failure:

- They aren't smart enough to resolve behavioral problems.
- They can't afford to spend money on their pets and therefore should never have gotten them in the first place.
- They don't care for their pets.
- Life means nothing to them.

Strong dependent adherents who apply the "what's good for my dog is good for me" attitude to euthanasia run smack into mercy killing, a very sensitive issue for most of us. When the time comes to make a decision for or against euthanasia, what can we say to the Grummonds, the Rossmans? If Dave Grummond continues treating Daisy even though he knows it's useless, he doesn't want it, and he can't afford it, he's bound to grow, first ambivalent, then resentful toward his dog. If the entire Rossman clan gets together and badgers Eleanor into having Clover put to sleep, laying a guilt trip on her—"You're making her suffer, Mom"; "She's more dead than alive"; "She's only a dog,"; "You're being selfish"—Eleanor may eventually give in, but she'll never feel comfortable with her choice.

When it comes to euthanasia, veterinarians may be helpful or detrimental. As individuals, they are no more immune to the emotional input of human beliefs and value judgments than anyone else. In general, vets may supply two forms of support by explaining: (a) the medical facts concerning the dog's chances for a quality life in its current state, and (b) the emotional and life-style implications of the animal's continued condition. Because of their own beliefs, some vets will only state the straight medical facts while others will offer both kinds of information. Some owners want only facts; others demand feelings and opinions; some want to be *told* what to do, others want to hear nothing at all. Learning the mechanics of this fearful sub-

ject can help a lot. Like Dave Grummond, make that difficult appointment and discuss your needs and limitations
openly with your vet. Some people find this easier to do
with the dog present; others prefer to leave the dog at
home.

Surprisingly, a lot of people postpone euthanizing a pet
they believe to be suffering because they think they *have*
to stay with the pet when it's done, that it's somehow disloyal or cowardly not to be there. Nonsense! Because
you're going to go on living and may even get a new dog
soon, it's much better that you get on with life than sim-
mer in a stew of guilt and remorse. Pay attention to your
needs and those of your family as well as to the comfort
and dignity of your pet. In my experience, the strength of
the need, not the form of the need, confirms the love the
person feels for the pet. Owners of pets that always act up
at the vet's can expect them to be difficult when it comes
to euthanasia. On the other hand, many animals that are
quite unmanageable in the owner's presence (often reacting to the owner's own fears) remain calm in the owner's
absence. In such cases, owners can do both themselves
and their dogs a favor by not being present.

In some primitive hunting cultures which hold a deep
reverence for life, a hunter beseeches the animal's spirit to
flee in the split second before he releases his arrow. When
the arrow hits, the hunter thanks the animal for its coop-
eration and contribution to his own life. Euthanasia need
not be a senseless or meaningless act. Aware of our own
needs and our dog's place in fulfilling those needs, we can
make the decision with confidence and dignity.

Coping with Grief

How individuals deal with grief is the subject of many
books. Dog owners in general do one of three things: they
vow never to get another pet, they get another pet as soon
as they recognize an older dog is failing or immediately

following the death of a younger one, or they spend a few weeks or even months adjusting to the loss. Those who vow never to have another dog invariably belong to the Independent or Dependent school of thought. Because their guilt or self-identification creates so much emotionalism when the pet becomes ill or dies, these individuals often find it simpler to avoid the situation altogether. Unlike Bonded believers, who view the end as merely a part of the entire relationship, Independent and Dependent adherents tend to be totally consumed by the death itself and its effect on them. Is it any wonder they don't want to go through it again?

Getting a new pup to ease the transition or lessen the grief can be extremely beneficial. A few words of caution however:

- Never get a pup with the idea of *replacing* an aging or deceased one. Get a different sex, a different breed, anything that will keep you from making comparisons. I have seen many cases where eight-week-old pups were compared to well-behaved twelve-year-olds and found sorely lacking, resulting in much owner disenchantment and frustration. It's easy to forget that old Shamrock wasn't always the perfect house dog.
- Never get a pup for someone else facing old age or death in their pet without thoroughly discussing your intentions beforehand. Although I'm against a surprise animal gift under any circumstances, it can be totally inappropriate when old age or death are factors. You may think Dad or Susie wants another dog just as much as you do, but that may not be the case. Don't force the issue.

Spending time reflecting on one's relationship with one's pet and thoughts about future pets can also be beneficial. If you've always worked and had a dog, you may want to see what it's like not to have to come home every evening to walk and feed a pet. You may want to use the interval to decide whether you want another dog; if so, can you train a young pup now that you're on the road more? Are you still as partial to big dogs now that you've been transferred to the city?

One of the best ways to handle grief is to concentrate on the good memories. Sure, the last two weeks with Daisy were tough on the Grummonds, but there are fourteen years of good times with her to recall. Sally Grummond remembers dressing Daisy up in doll clothes when she was a pup; their neighbor remembers telling her son to sit down and having Daisy immediately obey the command. Dave remembers the countless walks and conversations with his dog—about life, politics, and taxes—Daisy's always being at his side when he was sick or down, the feel of the dog's silky coat, the playful, almost maternal look in her soft brown eyes. Good memories, years of them, to share with family and friends to ease the passage through a difficult time—that's the final gift a Bonded relationship has to offer the weekend dog and its owner.

CHAPTER 14

The Double Bond

*T*he day his parents' divorce becomes final, ten-year-old Sean Iverson makes himself a peanut butter and jelly sandwich, fills his GI Joe canteen with lemonade, and heads into the woods with Siegfried. As Jill watches her son and the dog disappear, she longs to go with them. It's not that Sean won't be safe with the now well-trained Siegfried; it's just that she could do with some canine companionship herself today.

As part of her work on the hospital volunteer staff, Adele Metzger often sits outdoors with the patients. When her husband comes to pick Adele up, Trinket jumps out of the car and comes dashing into the group to greet everybody, tail going like a propeller. Adele is amazed by how much pleasure this simple act gives even the most depressed patient. She is even more amazed to discover how many of these people have pets of their own who are dearly missed and worried about. Adele wonders how this affects their recovery.

Every day Roger Barclay parks his Mercedes in his personal parking space behind the towering building that houses his office at an international conglomerate. Every day Roger makes countless decisions affecting the flow of millions of dollars and the lives of countless nameless people dependent on those dollars. His colleagues consider him a genius; his clients refer to him as a financial wizard.

Last night Roger's eleven-year-old English bulldog, Winston, died quietly in his sleep. Few people will ever know that's why, for the first time that anyone can remember, Roger Barclay took the day off.

Throughout this book we've focused on the way people relate to their dogs, particularly in terms of how that relationship affects the dog's health and behavior. However, no book on dog ownership is complete without exploring what that relationship means. What does it mean when we're gone all day working, attending meetings, chauffeuring Little Leaguers, or collecting for charities while our dogs sit home alone? Nothing, nothing *negative* at all—if the relationship is good.

Instead of using the word "relationship," let's think about it as a bond, the uniting of two unique beings to make a new unit that is far different from either one. It saddens me that many people think of a close bond between a person and an animal as something negative, an indication that that person can't relate to people. As we have seen, there are those with highly Dependent beliefs who do seem to want a child more than a dog. On the other hand, the existence of this extreme is no reason to be afraid to bond at all, to create the unnecessary species barriers exemplified by the Independent view.

Although bonds with all kinds of animals (and plants) are possible, the bond between person and dog is a particularly special one for many reasons. A major reason is that our dogs need us not only for food and shelter but also for love and companionship. Equally important, we know we need them, too. A while back I saw a pamphlet with a picture of a forlorn pup on the cover and an emotional title like "Victim or Victimized?" which discussed the way heartless, inhumane people leave pups alone all day. It said that these pups are invariably unhousebroken and destructive, which inevitably leads to owner abuse. It urged that such people not be allowed to have dogs.

In theory, this seems like a most humane approach, but let's look at the other side. If a person is willing to come home every day and clean up the mess, if he or she is willing to live with the odor of excrement plus chewed-up furnishings and doors, who are we to say that person doesn't deserve to own a dog? Isn't it just possible that these people's needs for companionship are so great they're willing to endure what many of us would consider intolerable living conditions for either man or beast? To be sure, the purpose of this book is to show that we and our dogs *don't* have to live that way, but the point is that the bond between person and dog is often so strong that *how* we're together is usually secondary in importance to the fact that we *are* together.

I've seen a lot of dogs and a lot of people and have my own idea about what makes this bond so special. I believe that for many of us, the relationship we have with our dogs epitomizes that which we hope to have with other human beings, a nonjudgmental view that says, "Sometimes you do things I don't understand and sometimes I'm sure I do things you don't understand, but that never affects how much I love and respect you as a unique being." When Sean Iverson takes Siegfried into the woods, he knows he can communicate things to his dog he could never say to his parents, such as how hurt and confused he is by their divorce, or maybe even that he hates them or wishes he were dead. He can say all these things and Siegfried will listen, never offering any condemnation, never telling Sean it's wrong to think such things about himself or his parents. When the anger explodes in what Sean considers un-manly tears, only Siegfried will know; and Siegfried's tongue and Sean's sleeve will remove all evidence of Sean's first encounter with love and disappointment be-fore the two of them return home in time for dinner.

Does it seem bizarre that we would project our highest human goals on another species? At first glance maybe so, but if you think about it for a while it makes sense. In many ways, most of the problems we've discussed in *The Weekend Dog* are the same ones that plague us as week-end people. We suffer from boredom and isolation in our work as computer programmers, assembly-line workers, tiny cogs in gigantic legal firms, human numbers in vast advertising conglomerates, mothers–chauffeurs–committee members shuttling from one activity to the next. We take our kids to McDonald's on payday because mealtimes usu-ally are hectic, thrown-together affairs. We ply them with Ataris and Adidas to make up for those hours we're gone. Sometimes when we're exhausted or our confidence is shaken, we lash out needlessly, more often out of fear than anger, like our fear-biting canine counterparts. As we grow older, we find it harder to work in the garden all weekend without feeling stiff when we drag out of bed to go to work Monday morning. We sense the changes of age and are often confused and frightened by them. We know we want to succeed more than we want to fail, to be healthy more than to be ill, to learn more than to be ignorant, and, above all, to be loved and needed.

For those who find themselves separated from their pets in nursing homes, hospitals, and other institutions, being cut off from this bond is bound to create negative effects. Adele's hospital patient who daily worries more about whether her pug is receiving its heartworm preventive medication than she does about taking her own medicine is jeopardizing her own health. There are countless others who refuse to enter nursing homes for needed care simply because they will not leave their pets. When such individuals are forced by family or social services to do so, they are inevitably depressed and unhappy. For many people, the reference point for a quality life is the dog; when they are separated from it, life itself lacks definition and deteriorates correspondingly. Fortunately, most health professionals now recognize the value of this bond and pets are becoming an increasingly vital part of any treatment regime.

Is the bond any less important to those of us who are hale and hearty, able to juggle careers, community work, and family obligations? Hardly. The bond is our stabilizer, the one thing we can count on in all the chaos. So what if sometimes the dog complicates our lives? The important thing is that the dog is one of the few individuals, if not the only one, that never makes us feel we're complicating its life. Unlike parents, children, or employers, who often take each oversight as a personal attack—"How *could* you forget your father's birthday?" "Mom, you *promised* you'd bring home pizza for dinner tonight!" "What do you *mean* the Howard accounts aren't ready yet?"— we can forget to medicate, feed, or walk the dog and it still flops down beside the bed or gives a reassuring lap that says *It's all right; I understand.* When Winston dies, Roger Barclay knows it's useless for him to go into work. Roger is not an emotional man: he's cool, efficient, and precise; he does not make mistakes. Only Winston knew that Roger is also a man capable of crying and loving very deeply. Did Winston's presence make Roger a better manager? No one can answer that but Roger. But the fact remains that there's no doubt in Roger's mind that the loss of Winston, the breaking of that special bond, has had a profound effect on him.

A common thread binding all forms of life is an attraction for those who want and need the same things we do. And if the things we want are so basic, so much a part of every fiber of this great fabric we call Life that they can be fulfilled by a member of another species, how powerful that need must be and how great its message. The need is love: the message most eloquently and simply enshrined in Christian philosophy: "In so much as you do it unto the least of these, you do it unto Me."

By beginning with a sound bond with a species of equal need and uniqueness on this earth, we learn about that which is ultimately available to all mankind.

Epilogue

Never before have dog owners faced the wide range of problems precipitated by our weekend society, but neither have they enjoyed as many creative tools with which to solve them. If building a special soundproof area for a barking dog seems excessive to you, you can always turn to dependable denning. Maybe your dad effectively disciplined his hunting dogs with a good swat, but you'll get even better results with setups and distraction training. While your aunt who's raised champion Great Danes for thirty years resorts to heavy dietary supplementation, you can choose completely nutritional commercial dog foods. Even if your dog has a pedigree a mile long and represents the last of a great line, you can spay or castrate it to make it a more suitable and happy pet within your lifestyle.

Rather than suffering guilt over not staying home with our pets, we weekend dog owners should take joy from the very special relationship our life-style allows. Happy, healthy dogs need quality time rather than a quantity of time spent with them. The bond requires patience, creativity, love, and knowledge of our dogs as well as our own needs, but it is a bond more than worth the effort of creating.

There will always be those days when the alarm doesn't go off and the dog doesn't get fed, when the decision to crate the dog or put it to sleep will test our strength and courage. But there will also be days when we lie on our slightly battered carpets with their faintly doggy odor, gently stroking our best friends. Sure, it would be nice to own an oriental rug, and tend our perfectly aligned flower beds again, but for the moment, this is the best, the way it's meant to be.

Reinhold Niebuhr is credited with a simple and beautiful prayer that seems especially relevant to weekend dog owners:

Lord, grant me the serenity to accept the things I cannot change, the courage to change the things I can, and the wisdom to know the difference.

Index